Functional Fitness

D0619770

Acknowledgements

I would like to thank Peter Green and Kieran Noonan for their assistance in this project.

Medical Disclaimer:

The Body Coach Series

Functional Fitness

Build Your Fittest Body Ever
with Australia's Body Coach®

Paul Collins

Yuma County Library District
2951 S. 21st Ave.
Yuma, AZ 85364
www.yumalibrary.org

Meyer & Meyer Sports

British Library Cataloguing in Publication Data
A catalogue record for this book is available from the British Library

Paul Collins
Functional Fitness
Maidenhead: Meyer & Meyer Sport (UK) Ltd., 2009
ISBN 978-1-84126-260-4

Aachen, Adelaide, Auckland, Budapest, Cape Town, Graz, Indianapolis,
Maidenhead, Olten (CH), Singapore, Toronto
Member of the World
Sport Publishers' Association (WSPA)
www.w-s-p-a.org

Printed and bound by: B.O.S.S Druck und Medien GmbH, Germany
ISBN 978-1-84126-260-4
E-Mail: info@m-m-sports.com
www.m-m-sports.com

Apr 2010

Contents

A Word from The Body Coach®

When I talk about building your fittest body ever – I mean it!

Functional Fitness incorporates a progressive approach to fitness that has you building strength upon strength, skill upon skill and movement upon movement. This approach provides a stable platform that allows you to master one exercise before moving on to the next. It also helps establish important motor skills that mirror sporting, physical activity, occupational and daily lifestyle patterns so movement becomes more efficient and the body works as one complete unit.

To describe a working model of Functional Fitness, I'd like to share an insight using an analogy of the martial arts grading system. In karate, for example, an athlete starts their training with a white belt whilst learning the foundational training techniques and movement skill patterns that provide the basis for further technical improvements to occur in the future. Learning these basic techniques is crucial in that it lays the platform for better neuromuscular control from which upper, mid and lower body movement patterns are improved. As movement skills improve over the subsequent months, the athlete is offered an opportunity to be graded on these skill levels and possibly receive a higher colored belt, if seen as competent, for their efforts. From this point, if successful, more technically advanced and demanding movement patterns and drills are introduced that progress from previously learnt skills.

In some instances though, an athlete may progress quicker than others through the grading system due to higher levels of flexibility or muscle control from other base training such as gymnastics or dance or similar that often imitates various movements or skills of karate. In relating this approach to Functional Fitness, some athletes may have never performed an activity before whilst others may be returning from a long lay-off but are quite competent, whereas others will find it more difficult and challenging. Either way, every athlete needs to progress through the exercise progressions from easy to intermediate and more advanced to ensure they have mastered each exercise, drill or technique before moving forwards. The major difference is that some athletes may be able to do this in weeks whilst others take many months. In addition, some athletes may be so much fitter than others and whilst they may be able to easily perform a specific exercise, they may be seen to lack the technical skills required before progressing on to the next drill. This is where quality of movement is highly important. I say this from personal experience in helping guide athletes from state to national level and onto Olympic and Paralympic medals in their chosen sport. Quite simply, the rewards come from those who grasp the concept of obtaining a **Functional Fitness Foundation** (FFF); those who apply this approach and believe in what they are doing whilst also progressing through the essential **6 Movement Patterns** including:

1. **Support**
2. **Push**
3. **Pull**
4. **Squat**
5. **Core**
6. **Movement Fitness**

In working with thousands of athletes and coaches in multiple sports as a Strength and Conditioning Coach, my proficiency lies in the ability to provide you with exercise progressions in a manner that supports your sport specific needs. This in turn allows you to function at more optimal levels in sports specific training and witness greater performance in the competitive sporting arena. So even though some athletes may be lifting more weight in the gym this doesn't necessarily make them a better athlete, it just means they can lift more weight. Whereas, those who regularly apply a **Functional Fitness Approach** will achieve better functional strength relative to one's body weight and specific movement needs.

Most importantly, those solely focused on improvements of general fitness and personal health will be rewarded for their efforts over time with a stronger, more coordinated and more responsive body with the hundreds of drills to choose from, including using one's own body weight along with **equipment** including:

- **Medicine Balls**
- **Kettlebells**
- **Fitness Balls**
- **Barbells**
- **Dumbbells**
- **Cable Machines**
- **Markers**

Functional Fitness offers a progression from isolated to compound and multiple response drills that will allow you to successfully progress one step at a time and build your fittest body ever.

I look forward to working with you!

Paul Collins
The Body Coach®

Definitions
FFA = Functional Fitness Approach
FFC = Functional Fitness Chain
FFF = Functional Fitness Foundation
FFM = Functional Fitness Method
FFP = Functional Fitness Progression

About the Author

Paul Collins, Australia's Personal Trainer™ is founder of The Body Coach® fitness products, books, DVD's and educational coaching systems – helping people to get fit, lose weight, look good and feel great. Coaching since age 14, Paul has personally trained world-class athletes and teams in a variety of sports from Track and Field, Squash, Rugby, Golf, Soccer and Tennis to members of the Australian World Championship Karate Team, Manly 1st Grade Rugby Union Team and members of the world-renowned Australian Olympic and Paralympic Swimming teams. Paul is an outstanding athlete is his own right, having played grade rugby league in the national competition, being an A-grade squash player, National Budokan Karate Champion and NSW State Masters Athletics Track & Field Champion.

A recipient of the prestigious 'Fitness Instructor of the Year Award' in Australia, Paul is regarded by his peers as the 'Trainers' Trainer' having educated thousands of fitness instructors and personal trainers and appearing in TV, radio and print media internationally. Over the past decade, Paul has presented to national sporting bodies including the Australian Track and Field Coaching Association, Australia Swimming Coaches and Teachers Association, Australian Rugby League, Australian Karate Federation and the Australian Fitness Industry as well as travelling to present a highly entertaining series of Corporate Health & Wellbeing Seminars for companies focused on a Body for Success™ in Life and in Business.

Paul holds a Bachelor of Physical Education degree from the Australian College of Physical Education. He is also a Certified Trainer and Assessor, Strength and Conditioning Coach with the Australian Sports Commission and Olympic Weight Lifting Club Power Coach with the Australian Weightlifting Federation. As a Certified Personal Trainer with Fitness Australia, Paul combines over two decades of experience as a talented athlete, coach and mentor for people of all age groups and ability levels in achieving their optimum potential.

In his free time, Paul enjoys competing in track and field, travelling, food and movies. He resides in Manly Beach, Sydney, Australia.

For more details visit: www.thebodycoach.com

Chapter 1

Functional Fitness refers to:
"An exercise approach that allows the participant to progressively improve strength, skill and motor coordination in a manner that ultimately imitates and assists the movement skills used in everyday sporting, occupational and daily lifestyle activities."
Paul Collins, 2009.

Functional Fitness Foundation – FFF

If sports, fitness, exercise, personal health or coaching are a passion of yours, then you'll appreciate Functional Fitness because it will show you functional exercise progressions for improving your knowledge, understanding and skill levels that will help take your fitness and strength to new heights. This is because Functional Fitness is designed to progress specific exercises, movements, drills and skills from easy to more challenging – referred to as Functional Fitness Progression (FFP) or Functional Fitness Chain (FFC). This includes mimicking various sport specific and daily lifestyle movement patterns and exercises that may start from a static isolated position and progress into a more dynamic compound movement pattern.

It's a great advantage in sport, occupational and daily lifestyle activities to have the stamina, strength and stability in the specific movement patterns being performed over and over again. The advantage itself relates to the body being able to work as a unit without the build up of isolated stress. This is acquired through the application of working on a Functional Fitness Foundation – FFF.

The "FFF" approach initially relates to technically mastering 'Six Key Exercises' and their variations as prerequisite skills that serve as the basis from which most other functional exercise movement patterns are built upon. In general, each movement pattern includes a collection of related skills on the basis of which functional exercise progression occurs. The objective is to master the technical aspects of each movement and their variations and build good body awareness that allows you to control and adjust your body position accordingly in exercise like a pro-golfer can adjust their swing, as shown on the following page.

The Six Key Exercises Include:

Exercise	Muscle Region	Movement	Element
1. Push-up	Upper Body	Compound	Push

Refer to page 58 for exercise description

Variables:
- Core – neutral spine or dish position (see Drill 3 and 4).
- Foot placement – close or wide.
- Feet position – ball of foot or feet pointed resting on toes (nails) or one leg raised.

External variations of the push-up exercise include:
- Upper body raised or challenged – Hands resting on fitness or medicine ball, hand grips, bench, swing gym, balance board or similar.
- Base of support raised – Feet or knees resting on fitness ball, bench, swing gym, balance board or similar.
- External resistance – one leg raised, weighted vest, resistance band, plate on back, partner resistance, time under tension, speed of movement, Plyometric push-up (concentric/eccentric).

All sports that include running, upper body involvement and impact based.

Exercise	Muscle Region	Movement	Element
2. Pull-ups	Upper Body	Compound	Pull

Refer to page 74 for exercise description

Variables:
- Hand placement – wide grip, reverse grip, cross-over grip.
- Angle of pull – vertical, diagonal.
- Core – neutral spine; dish position (see Drill 3 and 4) – a good indicator of core synergy whilst working back and arm muscles.
- Leg position – free hang with legs together and toes pointed or relaxed.
- Support – non-assisted or assisted (foot or knees supported).

External variations of the pull-up exercise include:
- External resistance such as: Weighted vest; weighted plate linked to belt.
- Rope Climbing.

Sports such as Swimming, Rock Climbing and Kayaking as well as those that involve the large back musculature.

Exercise	Muscle Region	Movement	Element
3. Body Dish - Supine	Core	Isolated/Static and/or Repetition	Core

Refer to page 103 for exercise description

Variables:
- Hand placement – hands across chest; hands extended overhead.
- Leg position – one leg bent and one leg raised; both legs raised – toes pointed.
- Angle of pull – abdominal contraction for obtaining dish position.
- Support – non-assisted or assisted (partner spotting legs and shoulders).

External variations of the Supine Body Dish exercise include:
- External resistance such as hand weights, ankle weights, partner pushing arms or legs for body rocking effect.
- Progression: Collins Rotational Pattern – 180-degree and 360 degree variations.

Sports such as gymnastics and diving, athletics, baseball, basketball, volleyball, cricket, tennis, netball, soccer, surfing and all contact sports for muscle control – AFL, NFL, NHL.
Position a good indicator of core body strength when performing exercises such as push-ups and pull-ups.

Exercise	Muscle Region	Movement	Element
4. Body Dish - Prone	Core/Upper Body	Isolated/Static	Support/Core

Description
- Start in front support position on hands and toes.
- Apply 3B's Principle™ - Brace, breathe and body position.
- Slowly extend hands forward 10cm (or 4-inches) at a time for a brief period 1-10 seconds whilst the torso moulds into reverse dish position.
- Keep movement of hands until inability to hold good body and shoulder position, sliding down to floor.

Variables:
- Hand placement – touching, close, wide grip, angled, extended to side.
- Core – neutral spine (start); reverse dish position (extended).
- Leg position – feet close, feet wide, one leg raised – toes always pointed.
- Support – non-assisted or assisted (1) toes resting against edge of wall (2) partner grasping hips to support load.

External variations of the Prone Body Dish exercise include:
- External resistance: In dish position, you hold a strong and stable body position whilst the coach pushes and pulls to try and put you off balance.
- Sports such as swimming that involve the large back muscles.
- Collins Rotational Pattern – 180-degree and 360-degree variations.

Strength in this position a good indicator of core body control when performing exercises such as push-ups and pull-ups as well as sprinting.

Exercise	Muscle Region	Movement	Element
5. Squat	Lower Body	Compound	Squat

Refer to page 84 for exercise description

Variables:
- Arm placement – forwards, crossed, waistline, holding weighted resistance.
- Technical positioning – ear line over shoulder, knees over toes in lowered position; weight resting on foot print to avoid ankle and kneeling rolling in or heel lifting.
- Movement – quarter, half, full squat and single leg variations.
- Support – non-assisted or assisted (fitness ball, smith machine or similar).

External variations of the Squat exercise include:
- External resistance such as weighted vest; dumbbell, barbell, kettlebell, medicine ball or similar.

Essential for all sports especially speed and power based.
Base exercise for leading into more powerful drills including jumping and landing and plyometrics.

Exercise	Muscle Region	Movement	Element
6. Lunge	Lower Body	Compound	Squat / Core

Refer to page 93 for exercise description

Variables:
- Arm placement – forwards, crossed, waistline, holding weighted resistance.
- Technical positioning – legs lunge to 90-degree angles; hips remain square.
- Movement – stationary, alternate leg, side, diagonal, backwards, raised – flat bench, unstable surface, lunge with rotation, walking, step ups, plyometrics, bounding.

External variations of the Squat exercise include:
- External resistance such as weighted vest; dumbbell, barbell, kettlebell, medicine ball or similar.

Essential for all sports, especially speed and power based.
Base exercise for leading into more powerful drills including jumping and landing, plyometrics and sprinting.

Terminology

- **Compound** relates to an exercise that involves two or more joint movements.
- **Isolated** is an exercise that involves just one discernible joint movement.
- Combining **isolated** and **static** together refers to holding a muscle in a static position relative to the desired body position.

Foundation Activities

Athletes can sometimes become frustrated in their attempts to perform a skill or exercise because they may lack the strength, endurance or range of mobility. All of these abilities will improve with time, focus and effort by adapting a Functional Fitness Progression (FFP). It is recommended that each athlete master the Six FFF exercises before moving on to more advanced drills or sequences.

Chapter 2

Coach Collins™ Functional Fitness Method (FFM)

Every good exercise program starts with a method upon which training principles are based. In my book **Awesome Abs** I devised a 5-Phase Abdominal Training System for maximizing your core potential. In **Speed for Sport**™ I devised a 6-Stage Fastfeet® Training Model for maximizing your speed potential. While in **Functional Fitness** I have devised the Functional Fitness Method (FFM) that includes 'Six Key Movement Patterns' that aim to provide a balance of muscular strength, fitness and mobility throughout multiple planes of motion for building your fittest body ever.

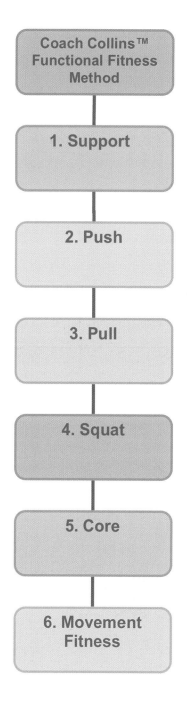

Coach Collins™ Functional Fitness Method

1. Support

2. Push

3. Pull

4. Squat

5. Core

6. Movement Fitness

Six Key Movement Patterns

Many of the skills incorporated within the six key movement elements progress from basic to intermediate and more advanced functional movement patterns. Many of the skills are simple lead-up activities which them-selves lead to more complex skills. The six key movement patterns all work together to mold functional fitness develop-ment. In some instances, you will find one element may override another. For instance, your push movements (ie. push-ups) may be strong whereas your pull movements (ie. pull-ups) are weak. The benefit of this is that the Coach Collins'™ Functional Fitness Method enables you to uncover your strengths and weaknesses and focus on regaining better body balance for building your fittest body ever.

The Six Key Movement Patterns are simply defined in terms of movement as described on the opposite page:

Movement Pattern 1: Support

Supports range from basic balance or static exercises on the hands, forearms, knees, feet or equipment. This includes isometric holds such as front supports, handstand, rear support, side support and single leg balance.

Movement Pattern 2: Push

When you perform push exercises, you carry out movements in which you push the weight or resistance away from your body, for example, a bodyweight push-up or the bench press exercise for the chest and arm muscles. The push exercises typically focus on the chest, shoulders, triceps, quadriceps and outer thighs.

Movement Pattern 3: Pull

When you perform pull exercises, you carry out movements that pull the weight or resistance towards you. The muscles worked include the back, biceps, gluteals and hamstrings.

Note: In some exercises, the load shift combines Elements 2 and 3 for push and pull movement patterns.

Movement Pattern 4: Squat

The squat is a Functional Fitness Foundation (FFF) compound exercise that that involves two or more joint movements which serves as the basis from which leg strength and power develop.

Movement Pattern 5: Core

The abdominal and lower back muscles combine to form the core region of the body. The core region helps stabilize the body for more efficient and effective movement patterns to occur between the upper and lower body. Exercises include both static isometric bracing drills as well as those that target the rectus abdominus and obliques through various angles and intensities.

Movement Pattern 6: Movement Fitness

Movement Fitness focuses on drills that include the use of multiple muscle groups in action. It relates to functional movement patterns that increase the heart rate in terms of agility, reaction, overspeed, medicine ball, speed endurance and plyometric power drills.

Functional Fitness Progression (FFP)

To effectively prescribe functional exercise progression, a number of external factors come into consideration when selecting exercises. These have been separated into two groups: Intensity and Technical. In general, the intensity aspect relates to an increasing load placed on the muscle or series of muscles whilst the technical aspect relates to the requirement of the movement itself – in some cases various elements mold between the two. The following table summarizes the functional exercise progression factors in your complete understanding of the functional fitness approach and future program design.

Functional Fitness Progression Table:

Intensity	Technical Aspect
• External Stimulus – Rotational patterns • External resistance • Lever Length Challenge – short to long • Mechanical stress – absolute weight being lifted • Gravity dependent • Exercise Intensity • Repetitions • Sets • Power • Time held under tension • Speed of movement (eg. 3:1:3 in a push-up exercise = 3 seconds down, 1 second hold, 3 seconds up) • Push, Pull or Static movement • Recovery • Load shift – shift of resistance through multiple muscle groups throughout the range of motion • Neuromuscular (Central Nervous System – CNS) demand and neuromuscular capability (too much too early may affect performance)	• Planes of motion – sagittal, frontal, horizontal • Angles of movement • Stationary to ongoing movement • Isolated to compound movements • Range of motion • Motor challenge • Bench: decline, flat, incline • Multiple movements • Travel (or movement from starting point) • Joint stability • Base of support – close or wide (hands or feet); stable or unstable (balance) • Proprioceptive awareness • Level of difficulty • Posture • Hand and arm positions • Equipment: dumbbell, barbell, kettlebell, medicine ball, fitness ball, cable machine, etc.

In light of the intensity and technical aspects involved in functional fitness progression from the chart on the previous page you can see how complex exercise selection can become. To help overcome this complexity, I have devised a table below that incorporates simple terminology as utilizing the Functional Fitness Approach (FFA).

Table: Functional Fitness Progression – Simple Terminology

Low Intensity	Moderate Intensity	High Intensity
Easy		Difficult/Complex
Isolated		Compound
Single Response		Multiple Response
Static		Plyometric

Functional Fitness Progression – FFP – Intensity and Technical Aspect

Functional Fitness Approach (FFA)

Applying a Functional Fitness Approach (FFA) requires good technique with correct body position maintained at all times whilst performing an exercise. To meet this need, there are two basic factors to consider in exercise selection:

1. If the exercise, weight or load, repetition or time selected result in early technique breakdown, the movement itself may be too demanding and must be modified to avoid poor movement mechanics.

2. At the other end of the spectrum, if the exercise does not cause a degree of fatigue then the exercise, weight or load, repetition or time selected, may need to be increased.

Whilst there are many factors that may contribute to technique breakdown, ultimately, the balance comes from understanding the **75-Percent Rule™**. This means that when performing an exercise, fatigue should start to rapidly occur at approximately the 75% mark of the desired set range, at which point a higher focus is required on maintaining correct body position whilst aiming to complete the movement. For example if the set amount of repetitions established is 12, then a rapid onset of fatigue should start to occur at around 9 repetitions until the 12th repetition is complete. The **75-Percent Rule™** aims to help guide you when exercising because if 12 reps are set and there's no real fatigue in the movement until this end point, then the exercise, weight or load, repetition or time selected needs to be modified. Other factors that may need to be considered in this equation include recovery time between sets and location of exercise within the training program itself.

In consideration of the **75-Percent Rule™,** when training an athlete I like to ensure a solid base is acquired first. Sometimes though there is a balance between a hard and easy exercise that needs to be considered. In light of this, I might have an athlete perform a demanding exercise and when fatigue sets in early (in the rep count) swap straight to an easier exercise of the same movement pattern to complete the set amount of repetitions – eg. from a push-up on the toes to a push-up on the knees. Let's refer to this as "Layer Training" which is a great way to introduce an athlete to a progressive exercise in the Functional Fitness Chain (FFC) by allowing the athlete to experience the next level of demand and build stamina by combining it with an easier exercise. This also helps improve an athlete's stamina (staying power), confidence and motivation levels by allowing them to perform a new exercise and, although falling short, providing them with the incentive to work harder to reach this new goal.

Progression Contradictions

In some instances, athletes may find one exercise easier than another to perform on the Functional Fitness Chain (FFC) due to such factors as limb length, training background, load and so forth as mentioned in the Functional Fitness Progression Table on page 23. The progression of exercises is designed as a reference guide from my coaching experience. By understanding the factors that contribute to functional exercise progression, you will understand that from time to time some exercises are similar in intensity but may require a higher technical aspect as opposed to a higher load. Feedback from a coach is therefore important to ensure that the athlete is performing the exercise correctly and maintaining good form. Remember, what is often seen as easy for one athlete may not be for another. Hence, the focus should be on the quality of movement at all times. As all exercises of the Functional Fitness Chain have multiple variables – ability to add weight or load – the exercise list in the upcoming chapters acts as a guide only.

Functional Mobility and Stability Variables

Confusion often arises in training circles when discussing the topics mobility and stability. To make things clearer I will discuss the roles that stability and mobility and their variables play as part of two areas:

1. **Warming up** – due to large variances in range of movement from athletes with muscular tension through to others with hypermobile joints
2. **Functional exercise progression variables**

Joint Stability

1. Warming up

All six of the key movement elements require good functional mobility and/or stability to enable you to perform exercise at your optimal potential. Athletes who are lacking flexibility, range of motion or growing older in age require a much longer warm-up period than most to ensure good blood flow and warmth to the working muscles, ligaments and joints for improving functional joint mobility. At the end of a training session, these athletes should ensure a good cool down period combined with a range of static and dynamic flexibility drills.

At the other end of the scale, athletes who are hypermobile in one joint or a series of joints require a higher focus on Element 1 with support based drills as well the FFF drills to ensure greater stability and proprioceptive body awareness of muscles and joints. In many instances, a hypermobile athlete should avoid stretching a hypermobile joint, instead spend more time warming up the body through stability based drills and technical range of movement drills focused on good muscular control.

Movement Variables	Warm-up Approach
1. Joint Stiffness (or age)	Longer warm-up period combined with focus on mobility drills
2. Good Mobility	Normal warm-up and stretch
3. hypermobile joint(s)	Warm-up involving stability drills for hypermobile joint(s); no stretching of these joints required

2. Functional exercise progression variables

In terms of describing stability before mobility in exercise, this refers to ensuring stability of a joint before adding mobility. This is extremely important for the hypermobile athlete. A range of static exercises that vary in positioning should be mastered to ensure that when a similar movement progression of a dynamic nature is introduced that the joint and muscle group(s) themselves can handle the training load, namely to increase strength and avoid injury. Element 1 and Element 5 focus on building base supportive strength that supports more dynamic movements.

One exercise scenario of adaptation to the functional progression approach in terms of stability upon mobility would include the push-up exercise as described below:

- As an athlete and coach I know that the ability to perform 50 push-ups without loss of form, with the hands in both a close and wide grip position is a good indication that more dynamic or plyometric push-up type movements can be introduced. This would progress over a period of time through a progression of static front support drills onto kneeling and full push-up type patterns including the use of fitness balls, medicine balls, balance boards and various hand grip equipment such as push-up handles, dip bars and so forth.
- The reference, "without loss of form" relates to one's ability to hold a strong core abdominal position without any sagging or aching of the lower back beyond just neutral spine position to include the dish hold position. This ensures good synergy between the upper, mid and lower body regions when aiming to introduce more powerful movements.
- Throughout the above instances the athlete can be introduced to more powerful movement patterns as individual steps or reps, such as performing medicine ball chest passes against a wall at a low intensity to build both concentric and eccentric strength endurance before increasing the intensity of the drill. It may also include a limited number of kneeling plyometric drops into a front support position for eccentric loading development with the ability to control and decelerate motion. And the list of similar supporting drills goes on.

By describing this above scenario, you can see where the stability before mobility approach fits in. But in saying this, a challenge of mobility combined with stability is the essential ingredient for ongoing development and a key element of training called having fun! Now, before I go any further let us get back to why it's important to being able to perform 50 push-ups with good form. Firstly, the more push-ups one performs the more strength endurance is increased. As strength endurance increases, the movement can be performed faster – improving speed, neuromuscular control and fitness levels through establishing better supportive strength. These elements are indicators that an athlete is able to progress forwards in functional fitness drills. When an athlete is introduced to new and more demanding exercises you'll see that the endurance of the exercises may be lacking and a development period is required to build the appropriate strength once more. This is because the demand on the muscles, surrounding tissues and energy systems requires time to adapt and improve and why repetitions, sets and recovery or time on task is applied.

At this point, as an athlete or coach you need to understand the importance of base development and ensuring that this is regularly tested and maintained over a training year. In terms of fitness for an athlete who requires speed in a team sport, regular jogging and speed endurance in combination with 'Pure Speed' training itself is the model for ensuring speed is maintained throughout the game period.

A person with a background in gymnastics for instance may contradict some of the above statements by easily being able to perform 50 push-ups, even after 5 or 10 years away from the sport. In these instances, a person's base needs to be considered as well as ensuring a base conditioning period is undertaken to allow the muscles, ligaments, tendons and energy systems to re-adapt to reduce any risk of injury when performing more dynamic movement patterns in the future. In saying this, how often do you see an athlete return to a sport after a long break and get injured. This is because, although they can easily perform the drill or skill, a preparatory period is required as a base for the body to adapt once again. So, if the gymnast can easily perform 50-push-ups they may require a 4-week preparatory period using the bench press exercise to establish this supportive strength before undertaking more dynamic exercises. Remember, not one exercise or scenario fits all. Each athlete will differ in their requirements and training approach. What I will provide you as we move throughout this book are a series of functional fitness progressions for the six key movement elements.

As an athlete or coach, your training experience will help guide you to where your starting point is and functional progressions to undertake. Whilst others new to this arena will start by progressing one exercise at a time applying the stability before mobility training approach before mingling stability and mobility drills (stability upon mobility) for more effective endurance, strength and power gains.

Sequences

The Functional Fitness Method is a progressive program of skills, drills, exercises and intensity – some in load and others in technical application. To assist in the transition between exercises, one focus is based on skill mastery – because once a skill is learnt the intensity (or load) can be increased. From another angle, some exercises may seem to have very little skill mastery and are progressed simply by increasing the load bearing of the exercise. Either way, all exercises have sequences and angles of difficulty that enable progression from basic to intermediate and more advanced levels. The emphasis is on confident body management.

Determining Repetitions and Sets

The ideal number of repetitions (reps) varies between 8-12 and 12-15 reps, for strength and endurance respectively, and 3 sets per exercise. As muscle needs to be overloaded to stimulate growth, in body weight training this is achieved through a core-strength continuum. In lifting weights you simply add more weight to the bar, whereas in body weight training you can increase the intensity or overload by slowing down the time it takes to perform each repetition (i.e. from 2 seconds to 4 seconds), otherwise performing a more challenging exercise for the same muscle group – the goal of the core-strength continuum. As one exercise becomes easy, you move up the core-strength continuum to a harder exercise of the same muscle group. This may entail going from performing a push-up on the ground to having the feet resting on a fitness ball to increase the challenge. In other cases, it may require starting with harder exercises first and easy exercises later in the training so you fall within this 8–12 repetition range as the exercises are much harder to perform from fatigue.

Overload in bodyweight training can also come from rotating exercises and reducing the rest periods between sets. Time on task can also be used as a replacement of repetitions. As not one routine fits all, having various options available provides the variety required to achieve your goal. Ultimately it becomes a game of trial and error, as some participants will easily surpass the set amount of reps, where others fail. So, aim for the 8–12 repetition range. If you do it easy, change the exercise or simply slow the exercise down you can spend more time under tension. For example, if you can do 12 push-ups easy in 12 seconds, slow it down to perform up to 12 reps in 24 or 36 seconds (2 or 3 seconds each rep) maintaining good form and you will be challenged. Ultimately, the variations supplied above will help establish the repetitions and sets to suit your needs for overloading a muscle group for optimal strength gains between muscle groups. Vary exercises regularly to maintain this challenge and always focus on improving the link between weaker and more dominant muscle groups throughout the body for better movement synergy.

Recovery or Rest Periods

Allowing 30–180 seconds recovery is recommended between most exercises, if working the same muscle group or the same exercise is being repeated. Recovery is generally based on two key elements:

1. Purpose of your training – low, medium or high intensity (endurance, strength or power based).
2. One's current fitness or strength level.

The longer the recovery period, the fresher you will be – choose accordingly.

Functional Fitness Training Tools

Functional fitness training often requires a combination of body weight with external resistance apparatus and sports training equipment. Here are some of the best equipment options for functional fitness training:

Body Weight
* Your own body weight can be used for many functional fitness exercises including pulling, pushing, isometric and more powerful plyometric movements.

Fitness Balls
* Fitness balls are good for helping to improve stability and balance.

Medicine Balls
* Medicine balls come in many different weights and an excellent tool for abdominal and power training.

Dumbbells
* Fixed or adjustable dumbbells allow you to add resistance to the hands for performing multiple angle drills.

Barbells
* Barbells are used for exercises such as squats and other compound exercises requiring strength and power.

Weight Plates
* The weight plate itself can become a great functional training tool in addition to the medicine ball by allowing you to work the resistance to your body at different angles with varying weights.

Cable Machine
* Pulley cables connected to adjustable weight plates that enable varying angles to be strengthened.

Kettlebells
* Cast iron weighted ball with handle designed for use in multiple power movements.

Markers
- Markers are used to set-up grids for various speed and agility drills as well as establishing distances and boundaries.

Speed Equipment
- Speed training equipment such as mini-hurdles, speed ladders and agility poles assist greatly in the development of quickness and agility.

"By applying these six key movements elements with my own athletes, I have been able to effectively build a solid foundation from which I can apply more advanced exercises of increasing difficulty to help improve athletic performance."
Coach Collins

Chapter 3

Muscle Movement

Anatomy of Movement

The body is divided into three anatomical planes – Sagittal, Frontal and Horizontal. The Sagittal plane divides the body down the center or vertically. The Frontal plane divides the body from front to back. The Horizontal plane divides upper and lower. The table below lists the anatomical term and the corresponding description.

Sternocleidomastoideus
Deltoids
Pectoralis Major
Biceps Brachii
Serratus Anterior
Rectus Abdominus
Obliques
Illopsoas
Adductors
Quadriceps
Tibialis Anterior

Trapecius
Deltoid
Teres Major
Tricepcs Brachii
Latissimus Dorsi
Forearm
Erector Spinae
Gluteus Medius
Gluteus Maximus
Hamstrings
Gastrocnemus
Soleus

Anatomical Term	Description
Anterior	Front
Medial	Inside
Posterior	Rear
Lateral	Outside
Supine	Face up
Unilateral	One side
Bilateral	Both sides
Prone	Face down
Superior	Upper
Inferior	Lower

Types of Muscle Contraction

While it is known that muscle fibers can only contract and shorten, as a whole they can develop a force in more than one way as shown below:

Isometric	Where the muscle tension and muscle length remain constant
Concentric	Where the muscle shorten as the fibers contract
Eccentric	Where the muscle lengthens as it develops tension
Isokinetic	Where the muscle contracts through its full range of movement

In each exercise there are four main functions of the associated muscles:

1. **Agonists** (prime movers) - generally refers to the muscle we are exercising.

2. **Antagonists** - is the opposing muscle and acts in contrast to the agonist.

3. **Stabilizers** - are those that hold a joint in place so that the exercise may be performed. The stabilizer muscles are not necessarily moving during exercise, but provide stationary support.

4. **Assistors** - help the Agonist muscle doing the work.

The following table lists muscles and their opposing counterparts. These columns are reversed when exercising muscle on the right hand column, for example, the Antagonist becomes the Agonist and visa versa:

Agonist (Prime Mover)	Antagonist
Biceps	Triceps
Deltoids	Latissimus Dorsi
Pectoralis Major	Trapezius/Rhomboids
Rectus Abdominis	Erector Spinae
Iliopsoas	Gluteus Maximus
Hip Adductor	Gluteus Medius
Quadriceps	Hamstrings
Tibialis Anterior	Gastrocnemius

In prescribing all six key movement patterns as part of the functional fitness program, it is important to have muscle balance to prevent injury. Muscular balance refers to the relationship between the Agonist and Antagonist. If the Agonist is much stronger than the Antagonist (or visa versa) the Agonist can overpower the Antagonist and cause injury.

Joint Actions

Muscular joints of the body provide a fulcrum point for muscles to be worked. There are six types of joint actions. In the table below I will describe the movement and example exercise:

Joint Action	Movement Description	Example Movement
Flexion	Decreasing joint angle	Biceps Curl
Extension	Increasing joint angle	Leg Extension
Abduction	Movement away from the body midline	Deltoid Lateral Raises
Adduction	Movement toward the body midline	Horizontal Chest Flyes
Rotation	Rotation about an axis	Twisting the Arm
Circumduction	360 degree rotation	Circling the arm around

Applying the 3B's Principle™

Every exercise has a number of key elements to consider when setting up and performing a movement. Applying correct technique from the onset will help establish good form which is ultimately maintained until the repetitions or set is completed, before relaxing. After reviewing Anatomy of Movement, the key elements required in order to maintain good body position whilst exercising form part of a simple exercise set-up phrase I've called the **3B's Principle™**:

1. **Brace**
2. **Breath**
3. **Body Position**

I will expand on their roles collectively below:

1. Brace

Activating and bracing your abdominal muscles whilst exercising is important because it helps increase awareness of your body position as well as helping unload the stress on the lower back region. For an effective abdominal brace whilst exercising, one should initiate the brace whilst maintaining the natural curvature of one's spine, known as the neutral spine position. Simply, think of a gymnast or dancer holding a tall proud body posture. Now in this position, draw the abdominal muscles inwards to approximately 30-50% of maximum contraction whilst continuing to breathe deeply. Initially, breathing may feel short and shallow, yet overtime through regular practice your lung capacity will improve whilst maintaining a solid body position. The abdominal brace itself also plays a key role in helping protect the lower back by distributing the load throughout the core region.

Abdominal Bracing in association with neutral spine position holds an important role in maintaining good posture and can be performed in sitting, lying, kneeling, standing and range of movement exercises.

To get started, sit tall in a chair, bracing your abdominals and taking 5-deep breaths in and out without the abdominal muscles moving. Breathe in through the nose and out through the mouth adjusting the brace (hold) for further stomach contraction. As your lung capacity and bracing ability improves apply this to more demanding exercises involving use of the arms and limbs such as push-ups, for example, and see how more efficient the movement becomes.

The term 3B's Principle™ incorporating abdominal bracing, breathing and body position combinations will be referred to throughout this book as a reference point as most exercises – for example, think of finding neutral spine position, bracing your abdominal muscles and breathing deeply whilst maintaining a good body position the whole time whilst exercising by constantly re-adjusting. Practised regularly, the 3B's Principle™ will naturally activate when exercising.

2. Breathing

Throughout normal everyday activities, the nervous system usually controls respirations automatically to meet the body's demands without our conscious concern. When we are passive, or at rest, our demands for oxygen are small and breathing is slow and shallow. When there is an increased demand for oxygen, breathing becomes much deeper and swifter. When you start to exercise or move more rapidly, carbon dioxide from the muscle is pushed into the blood. This triggers a signal in the brain to make you breathe faster and deeper so that you supply more oxygenated blood to your working muscles.

One of the main functions of your respiratory system is to get oxygen from the air into the blood stream, and then expel carbon dioxide waste from the blood out into the atmosphere. Although the basic rhythm of respiration is set and coordinated by the respiratory center (neurologically), the rhythm can be modified in response to the demands of the body. In other words, breathing can be controlled voluntarily to some extent through conscious concern.

To maximize training results, draw in air deeply through the nose and out through the mouth through pursed lips (like blowing out candles) for a count of three. Deep breathing is practiced whilst maintaining neutral spine position, abdominal bracing and exercising. In general, you **Breathe out** when you exert a force (e.g. rise up in push-up exercise) and **Breathe in** with recovery (eg. lower down in push-up exercise)

This type of breathing results in the lungs being able to take in more air in a controlled manner. As more oxygen is taken into the bloodstream, the muscle's waste product carbon dioxide is expelled more efficiently, especially as you become fitter. The breathing focus when performing Functional Fitness Exercises is to control the rhythm of one's oxygen supply by being conscious of one's breathing patterns at all times whilst bracing and maintaining good body position like that of a ballet dancer.

3. Body Position

The third B in this equation relates to one's ability to hold a good body position – *neutral spine, effective abdominal brace and breathing pattern* – whilst exercising. By adapting the 3B's Principle™ you will build a unique internal understanding of your body, its muscles and how they respond to various movement patterns. Adapting the posture of a ballet dancer provides a good visual image of what is required in terms of maintaining a good body position whilst exercising.

In terms of Functional Fitness, as one's bracing ability and core strength levels improve, external movement patterns are introduced that increase the demand on these qualities. For example, as strength of the chest and arms improves performing a kneeling push-up, the intensity is increased to a full push-up on the hands and feet by extending the lever length. This itself increases the bracing demand of the abdominal region whilst reducing the load on the lower back. Then as breathing intensity increases, the aim is to maintain a good body position on an ongoing basis until the repetitions are completed. Ultimately, it doesn't matter what exercise you are performing, the aim is that the primary target muscles fatigue prior to the abdominal brace. This ensures a good body position is maintained at all times, optimizing one's training objectives.

As you progress through the exercises and principles outlined, you will begin to develop a unique understanding of your body, its movement and muscle control in space and time. In all exercises, ensure good head, neck, spine and pelvic alignment is maintained at all times with the rest of the body for the development of good posture. The overall focus of each exercise should therefore be on quality of the movement.

Applying the 3B's Principle™:

In the power push-up exercise below I will demonstrate how effective this simple application works. Setting up in the front support position, I find neutral spine position and brace the abdominal muscles to maximize core control and body position. Initiating the deep breathing pattern, I breath-in as I lower the body towards the ground and breathe out as I explode my upper body off the ground clapping the hands in mid air. Most importantly, whilst in mid air I maintain a good body position before landing and absorbing the stress by maintaining the 3B's Principle™ and repeating the exercise. In saying this, the moment the 3B's Principle™ is lost, the exercise is stopped, whether after just one repetition or 10.

Starting position that includes bracing and good body position.

Upper body explosion whilst breathing out and maintaining good body position through the application of the 3B's Principle™ ensures good form at all times. The exercise is stopped when form lapses.

So, next time you perform any exercise, simply apply the 3B's Principle™- Brace, Breath and Body Position for more effective functional fitness gains.

Chapter 4

Movement Pattern 1

Support

Isometric 'Support' Strength Exercises

Objective
- Improving joint stability, isometric static strength endurance and proprioceptive awareness in various support positions

In exercise, being able to hold a static body position effectively improves postural awareness, strength and muscle control. With the assistance of the 3B's Principle™ your goal with each exercise is to monitor and constantly readjust to hold the appropriate body position whilst maximizing the time the muscle is held under tension for appropriate stability 'support' improvement to occur. In most exercises the challenge is placed upon muscles and their associated joints. The challenge comes from being able to hold the core region and joints in their neutral position whilst fatigue sets in throughout the body. Isometric support exercises themselves provide an important role in functional fitness progression and are used to improve the neuromuscular link and proprioceptive awareness of the body.

1a. Front Support

Instructions

- Place hands under shoulders with head forward of finger tips and feet together.
- Apply 3B's Principle™ - brace abdominal muscles and ensure neutral spine position is held from the lower back to the head and neck.
- Hold strong body position as you continue to breathe deeply in and out for set period of time (i.e. 10-60 seconds or more).
- Utilizing the 3B's principle, continually make small body adjustments as required to maintain good body alignment at all times, especially contraction of the abdominal muscles.

Front Support – Functional Progression

The functional challenge is progressed through a range of exercises as follows:

1b. Rest lower body on pointed toes (nails)

1c. Raise one leg

- Normal foot position
- Toes pointed

1d. Feet Raised on Fitness Ball

Variables
- Rest on thighs
- Rest on shins
- Rest on dorsi-flexed toes
- Rest on pointed toes

Note: This exercise may actively progress by bringing knees to chest on fitness ball.

1e. Single leg balance

- Repeat the variables in 1d with one leg raised off the ball
- Fitness ball walk-out drill (active movement)

1f. Hands resting on unstable surface: Fitness ball, medicine ball, foam roller, balance board and alike utilizing drills 1a-1c. Once these are mastered, applying same principle with 1d and 1e under guidance of coach.

2a. Forearm Support

Instruction
- Start in a Front Support position, resting on elbows and forearms with clenched fists on the ground.
- Lean the body forward until eye line is over clenched fists. This ensures strong shoulder position.
- Brace abdominal muscles and ensure neutral spine position is held from the lower back to the head and neck.
- Hold strong body position as you continue to breathe deeply in and out for set period of time (i.e. 10-60 seconds or more).
- Utilizing the 3B's principle, continually make small body adjustments as required to maintain good body alignment at all times, especially contraction of the abdominal muscles.

2b. Variable: Raise one leg off ground to increase challenge

Forearm Support – Functional Progression

The forearm functional progression includes the Forearm to Front Support drill as follows:

2c. Forearm balance on fitness ball

- Start on knees before raising up onto toes.
- Raise one foot slightly off the ground.
- Try forearm support on other balance equipment.

Note: This exercise may progress onto an active kneeling prone roll out drill.

2d. Prone elbow to front support

- Starting on forearms, raise up onto one hand and then the other – into a front support position – before repeating movement in the opposite direction back down onto forearms.
- Keep abdominal muscles braced, shoulders square and avoid any hip movement.

3a. Rear Support

Instructions
- Sit on ground with hands behind body and pointed out to the side and legs extended, feet together and toes pointed.
- Raise hips up and hold extended position with strong abdominal brace and deep breathing pattern until loss of form, whether 3 or 30 seconds, then lower and stretch.
- Ensure body alignment and deep breathing pattern is maintained throughout holding pattern.

3b. Variable: Raise one leg off the ground.

Rear Support – Functional Progression

The functional challenge is progressed through a range of exercises as follows using a Body Coach® Fitness Ball:

3c. Fitness Ball Rear Support Hold – arms at 45-degrees

- Rest feet on fitness ball and arms out to side at 45-degree angle.
- Raise hips and hold body position with good form.

Note: This exercise may progress onto a fitness ball hamstring curl exercise.

3d. Fitness Ball Rear Support Hold – rest on elbows with fingers raised

3e. Fitness Ball Rear Support Hold – arms across chest

4a. Side Support

Instruction

- Lie on your side with the upper body supported by the elbow (90 degrees, directly below shoulder), forearm and clenched fist.
- Lower body supported by feet – positioned together along with legs.
- Lift the pelvis off the ground, eliminating the side bending by raising onto the edge of shoes or feet, forming a straight line from the feet to head – maintaining a neutral position and extend arm overhead.
- Rise up and hold body position for 10-30 seconds or more.
- Repeat drill on opposite side.

4b. Variable: Upper Arm vertical.

Note: This exercise can also be performed in a kneeling position.

Side Support – Functional Progression

The functional challenge is progressed through a range of exercises including the Collins Lateral Fly™:

4c. Side Support – 1 leg raised
- Raise upper leg and hold.
- Repeat opposite side.

4d. Hand on hip
- Place hand on hip.
- In addition, raise the upper leg and hold.
- Repeat opposite side.

4e. Collins Lateral Fly™
- Lower and raise slightly bent arm.
- Add hand weight to increase intensity.
- In addition to adding hand weight, raise upper leg and lower and raise arm.

5a. Hand Support - Handstand

Instruction
- Stand 1-2 meters from wall with both arms raised.
- Step forwards, bend at hips, place hands onto ground shoulder-width apart next to wall and drive legs up keeping body straight.
- Lean body against wall.
- Regularly adjust core abdominal region to keep body in good alignment.
- Maintain deep breathing pattern.
- Before fatigue sets in, push legs off wall onto ground and stand back up.

Note: All handstand variations require a qualified coach present to instruct and support.

Hand Support – Functional Progression

The functional challenge is progressed through a range of exercises including hand support holds and handstand variations:

5b. Arm Hold Sequence 1 – Balance (Crab hold)

- In a squat position, rest elbows on inside of knees.
- Lean body forward on ground and balance on hands.

5c. Arm Hold Sequence 2 – Balance

- As an active progression to 5b, brace abdominals and kick legs up and out into front support position.

5d. Vertical Wall Climb

- Start with feet to wall and head and hands away.
- Walk feet up wall to 45-degree angle and hold; 70-degree angle and hold; vertical and hold (only with coach present for support).

5e. Variable: Crab hold to 60-degree vertical hold with bent arms
5f. Variable: Crab hold to vertical handstand hold with straight arms
5g. Variable: Handstand push-ups against wall (see 5a) – active progression

6a. Balance Support - Single Leg

Instruction
- Stand with feet together and arms by side.
- Apply 3B's Principle™.
- Flex at hip and lean forwards resting on slightly bent leg.
- Raise one leg up behind keeping hips square, back flat until parallel to ground and arms pointing towards ground.
- Maintain good body position by regularly re-adjusting hip, leg and foot whilst balancing.
- Before fatigue sets in, raise body up and repeat with opposite leg.

6b. Variable: Add hand weights to 6a.

6c. Variable: Perform 6a. with arms raised out to side, parallel to ground.

6d. Variable: Fitness Ball Balances – sitting, lying, kneeling.

6e. Variable: Balance equipment: balances on wobble board or similar equipment.

Chapter 5

Movement Pattern 2

Push

Functional Chest and Triceps Progression

Chest Region
- Large fan shaped muscle that covers the front of the upper chest with a role of horizontal adduction, adduct, flex and inwardly rotate arm is called the pectoralis muscle.

Triceps
- The muscle at the back of the upper arm that extends the elbow.

The basic rule for most chest exercises is the narrower the hand position, the greater the triceps contribution and the lesser the chest contribution; conversely, the wider the elbow and hand position, the greater the chest contribution and the lesser the triceps contribution. The following exercises focus on the Movement Pattern = Push.

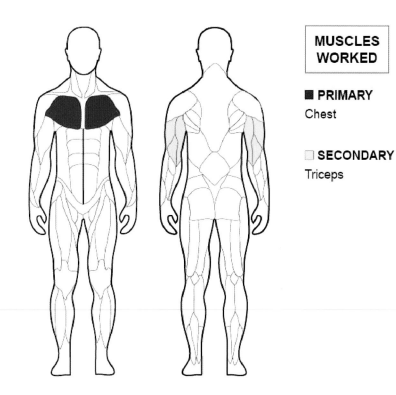

MUSCLES WORKED

■ **PRIMARY**
Chest

☐ **SECONDARY**
Triceps

Key Push Exercise = Push-Up

Instruction

- Start in a front support position – hands under shoulders, body leaning slightly forward with eye line directly over fingernails and abdominal muscles braced.
- Apply 3B's Principle™.
- Ensure neutral spine position is maintained from strong abdominal brace to avoid lower back sagging.
- Also ensure head and neck alignment is maintained at all times with the rest of the body for the development of good posture.
- Breathing in, bend at the elbows and slowly lower the body towards the ground.
- Keeping the elbows close to the body, breathe out as you straighten the arms.

Functional Fitness Progressions - low to high intensity.

Apply 3B's Principle™ with each exercise. Refer to Functional Fitness Progression Table (on page 23) for additional variations of intensity and technical aspects for these exercises:

Kneeling Close Grip Push-Ups
Rest on knees and hands. Keep elbows close to the body when lowering and raising.

Kneeling Close Grip Knuckle Push-Ups
Rest on knees and knuckles. Keep elbows close to the body when lowering and raising.

Two-finger Push-Ups
Rest on knees and 2 fingers (index and thumb). Keep elbows close to the body when lowering and raising.

Kneeling Wide Grip Push-Ups
Rest on knees and hands with wide grip when lowering and raising.

Close Grip Push-Ups
Rest on feet and hands. Keep elbows close to the body when lowering and raising.

Close Grip Knuckles Push-Ups
Rest on feet and knuckles. Keep elbows close to the body when lowering and raising.

Push-Ups
Rest on knees and hands with wide grip when lowering and raising.

Triangle Push-Ups
Rest on feet and hands with fingers and thumbs touching in triangle position under chest whilst lowering and raising.

Split Grip Push-Ups
Rest on knees and hands with split grip (one hand forward, the other back) when lowering and raising.

Fitness Ball Incline Push-Ups
Place hands on fitness ball and lower and raise body.

Fitness Ball Decline Knuckle Push-Ups
Place feet on fitness ball and knuckles on ground and lower and raise body.

Fitness Ball Decline Push-Ups
Place feet on fitness ball and hands on ground and lower and raise body.

Medicine Ball Push-Up on Knees

Rest on knees and place hands on medicine ball under chest and lower and raise body.

Medicine Ball Push-Up

Rest on toes and place hands on medicine ball under chest and lower and raise body.

Diagonal Push-Up

Rest on toes, with one hand on medicine ball and other hand on the ground and lower and raise body. Repeat opposite side.

Parallel Dips

Position hands on parallel dip bar and lower arms to 90-degree angle before raising.

Chest Dips

Position hands on parallel dip bar and flex at hip until 90-degree angle. Lower arms to 90-degree angle before raising.

Dumbbell Chest Press

Lie on bench on back with dumbbells resting at chest height shoulder-width apart. Extend dumbbells up above chest then lower.
Variation: Incline

Dumbbell Fly's

Lie on bench on back holding dumbbells in hands at full extension above chest with palms facing each other. Lower dumbbells out to side with slightly bent arms before raising up again.
Variation: Incline

Plyo Cross-over

Rest on toes, with one hand on medicine ball and other hand on the ground. Push-up and across swapping hands on ball.

Power Push-Up

Rest on toes, with both hands positioned on medicine ball. Push-up and off ball dropping hands into wide grip position on ground before exploding back up onto ball again.

Plyo Push-Up: Eccentric only

Rest on knees with arms extended forwards. Lean forwards and drop onto hands and absorb load by bending arms.

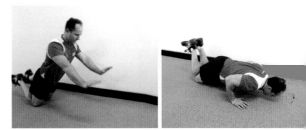

Plyo Push-Up

Rest on knees with arms extended forwards. Lean forwards and drop onto hands before rapidly pushing back up to starting position.

Kneeling Medicine Ball Push with Eccentric Landing

Rest on knees holding medicine ball at chest height. Explode ball from hands forwards of the body dropping down into kneeling push-up position.

Power Clap Push-Up

Rest on knees and hands with wide grip. Lower chest to floor then explode chest up off the ground and clap hands before landing and repeating.

Bench Press

Lie on bench holding barbell in extend position above chest with grip shoulder-width apart. Lower bar to chest before extending arms back to starting position. Vary tempo of movement for increases of intensity and strength and power requirements.

Variation: Incline bench; decline bench; Close grip (triceps); Follow bench press set with push-ups on ground or Plyometric drill.

Push-up Response – imitating sports movements

Start in lowered front support position and on coaches call push up off ground with a rapid response and sprint forwards for set distance.

See The Body Coach® Core-Strength Book for additional core-strength exercise variations.

Functional Shoulder-Specific Progression

Deltoids

The deltoids muscle has three parts:

1. Anterior deltoid (front) – draws arm forward, inwardly rotates and abducts arm
2. Medial deltoid (lateral) – Abducts arm
3. Posterior deltoid (rear) – draw arm back and abduct arm

The following exercises progress from pull to primarily focus on the Movement Pattern = Push.

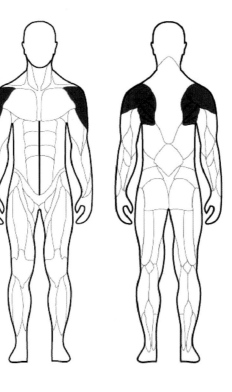

MUSCLES WORKED

■ **PRIMARY**
Shoulders

☐ **SECONDARY**

Functional Fitness Progressions - low to high intensity.

Apply 3B's Principle™ with each exercise. Refer to Functional Fitness Progression Table (on page 23) for additional variations of intensity and technical aspects for these exercises:

Single Arm Dumbbell Raises
Stand with feet shoulder-width apart and arms extended down in front of thighs holding dumbbells. Raise one arm up forwards until parallel to ground then lower and repeat with opposite arm.

Front Dumbbell Raises
Stand with feet shoulder-width apart and arms extended down in front of thighs holding dumbbells. Raise both arms up forwards until parallel to ground then lower.

Lateral Raises
Stand with feet shoulder-width apart and arms extended down in front of thighs holding dumbbells with palms facing together. Raise both arms out the side until parallel to ground then lower.

Rear Deltoid Flyes
Stand with feet shoulder-width apart, legs bent and hips flexed with arms slightly bent also and extended down in front of knees holding dumbbells – palms together. Raise both arms up to side leading with elbows to full range then lower.

Standing Overhead Press - Front

Stand with feet shoulder-width apart. Rest barbell across front of shoulders. Push barbell upwards overhead to full extension, then lower.

Barbell Push Press – Behind Neck

Stand with feet shoulder-width apart. Rest barbell across rear of shoulders. Push barbell upwards overhead to full extension, then lower.

Biceps Curls to Shoulder Thrust

Stand with feet shoulder-width apart with arms down by side holding dumbbells. Perform biceps curl with both hands before pressing dumbbells up overhead, before reversing the sequence going down.

Barbell Push Press – Rear

Stand with feet shoulder-width apart. Rest barbell across rear of shoulders. Perform a quarter squat then push barbell upwards overhead to full extension, then lower.

Barbell Push Press – Front
Stand with feet shoulder-width apart. Rest barbell across front of shoulders. Perform a quarter squat then push barbell upwards overhead to full extension, then lower.

Split Jerk
Stand with feet shoulder-width apart. Rest barbell across front of shoulders. Perform a quarter squat then push barbell upwards over-head to full extension with legs jumping into lunge position. Step front forward back, rear leg forwards and lower weight.

Reverse Wall Climb
Start facing away from wall on hands. Wall feet up wall until body vertical. Hold briefly, then walk hands back out away from wall and lower body.

Handstand with Wall Push-Up
Perform handstand against wall. Maintaining a strong body position bend elbows and lower head near ground then raise up to full extension again.

Note: Dumbbells can also be used in addition to all barbell power exercises shown above

Chapter 6

Movement Pattern 3

Pull

Functional Back and Biceps Progression

To work the large back region and supporting muscles you need to work them at a range of different angles. The following exercises focus on the Movement Pattern = Pull.

Latissimus Dorsi
- Large muscles of the mid-back that adduct, draw back (extend) and inwardly rotate arm.

Rhomboids
- Muscles in the middle of the upper back that brace and rotate scapula and pull it towards spine.

Trapezius (upper, mid, lower)
- Upper portion of the back, sometimes referred to as 'traps' that stabilize the scapula. Pull scapula towards the spine, some elevation, rotation and adduction. Upper part of traps can also extend and rotate neck.

Biceps
- The front of the upper arm – strong flexor and supinator of forearm.

Deltoids
- Posterior deltoid (rear) – draw arm back and abduct arm.

The following exercises target the back, rear deltoid and arm muscles.

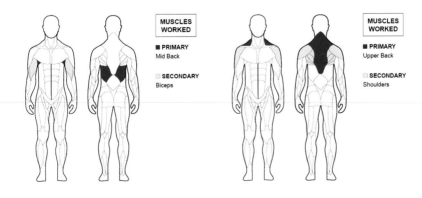

MUSCLES WORKED

■ PRIMARY
Mid Back

☐ SECONDARY
Biceps

MUSCLES WORKED

■ PRIMARY
Upper Back

☐ SECONDARY
Shoulders

Functional Fitness Progressions - low to high intensity.

Apply 3B's Principle™ with each exercise. Refer to Functional Fitness Progression Table (on page 23) for additional variations of intensity and technical aspects for these exercises:

Pull-Downs
Extend arms forward and parallel to ground holding cable bar attachment. Keeping arms straight, breath out as you pull bar down towards thighs, then up again.

Front Lat Pull-Downs
Kneel on ground in front of cable machine holding overhead bar. Lean sightly back as you pull the bar down towards chest, before raising.
Variation: Seated (machine)

Reverse Grip Pulls
Kneel on ground in front of cable machine gripping overhead bar with reverse hand grip shoulder-width apart. Lean sightly back as you pull the bar down towards chest, before raising.
Variation: Seated (machine)

Single Arm Row
Kneel on bench with one arm extended down holding dumbbell. Raise dumbbell up keeping elbow close to the body, then lower. Repeat drill with opposite arm.

Low Row
Sit on ground in front of cable machine with feet resting against supports and hands holding close grip handles in forward extended position. Slightly lean back whilst pulling both hands back towards stomach, before returning.
Variation: Single arm only

Bent Over Row
Stand with feet shoulder-width apart, legs bent and hips flexed with arms extended down in front of body holding barbell. In a rowing motion, pull barbell up leading with elbows to full range then lower.
Variation: High bench pulls

Pull Ups
Lie under fixed bar, set at waist height, with wide grip, arms extended and body held at 45-degree angle resting on heels. Pull body up to bar to chest then lower.
Note: Adjust body position to suit chest directly under bar.

Wide Grip Chin-Up

Grip overhead bar in wide grip position. Dish core region and pull body up with chin to bar then lower.

Note: Use bench for support to assist with drill whilst developing strength as well as holding top position for set period of time.

Reverse Grip Chin-Up

Grip overhead bar with close grip reverse hand position – palms facing body. Dish core region and pull body up with chin to bar then lower.

Note: Use bench for support to assist with drill whilst developing strength.

Side Chin-Up

Positioned sideways to overhead bar, place one hand in front of the other. Dish core region and pull body up to one side of bar, lower, then up to the other side.

Note: Use bench for support to assist with drill whilst developing strength. Reverse grip also between sets.

Bag Pull Ups

Grip overhead boxing bag or similar with body fully extended. Pull body up until chin reaches hands, then lower.

Variation:

* Rope Climb
* Rock Climbing

Functional Hamstrings Progression

Hamstrings

- This is the group of muscles on the backside of the upper leg, running from the hip joint to the knee joint. Their primary function is to facilitate flexion of legs, medial and lateral rotation – important for walking, running and jumping.

The following exercises target the hamstrings and include gluteal and lower back regions.

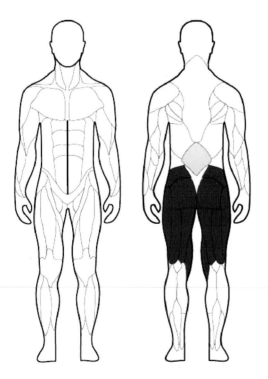

MUSCLES WORKED

■ **PRIMARY**
Glutes
Hamstrings

☐ **SECONDARY**
Lower Back

Functional Fitness Progressions - low to high intensity.

Apply 3B's Principle™ with each exercise. Refer to Functional Fitness Progression Table (on page 23) for additional variations of intensity and technical aspects for these exercises:

Body Weight Single Leg Dead-lift

Stand with feet together and arms by side. Flex at hip and lean forwards raising one leg up behind, keeping the other balancing leg slightly bent until body is parallel to ground, before returning to upright position. Repeat exercise with opposite leg.

Single Leg Dead-Lift with Dumbbells

Stand with feet together and arms by side holding dumbbells. Flex at hip and lean forwards raising one leg up behind, keeping the other balancing leg slightly bent until body is parallel to ground, before returning to upright position. Repeat exercise with opposite leg.

Cable Kick Backs

Place attachment from cable machine around ankle and step back away with trailing leg whilst holding support bar and raising up onto toes. Keeping body straight, kick forward leg and heel back keeping hips square at all times, before returning. Repeat drill with opposite leg.

Hamstrings Bridge

Lie on back on ground with bent legs, arms out to side resting on heels. Breathing out, raise hips off the ground until body is straight, then lower.

Single Leg Hamstrings Bridge

Lie on back on ground with one leg bent, resting on heel – close to the body – and the other leg extended and raised, with arms resting out to the side. Breathing out, raise hips off the ground until body is straight, then lower. Ensure hips remain square. Repeat with opposite leg.

Raised Hamstrings Bridge

Lie on back on ground with bent legs and heels resting up on flat bench, with arms out to the side. Breathing out, raise hips off the ground until body is straight, then lower.

Raised Single Leg Hamstrings Bridge

Lie on back on ground with one leg bent, resting on heel on flat bench and the other leg extended and raised, with arms resting out to the side. Breathing out, raise hips off the ground until body is straight, then lower. Ensure hips remain square. Repeat with opposite leg.

Fitness Ball Hamstrings Bridge

Lie on back on ground with bent legs and heels resting up on fitness ball, with arms out to the side. Breathing out, raise hips off the ground until body is straight, then lower. Ensure hips remain square.

Single Leg Fitness Ball Hamstrings Bridge

Lie on back on ground with bent legs and one heel resting up on fitness ball and other leg straight, with arms out to the side. Breathing out, raise hips off the ground until body is straight, then lower. Ensure hips remain square.

Fitness Ball Hamstrings Curl

Lie on back with feet raised up on fitness ball, resting on heels and arms out to the side. Breathing out, draw heels towards buttocks by bending knees before extending legs out again. Ensure hips remain square and heels firmly pushed into the ball.

Leg Curl

Lie on stomach in leg curl machine and kick heels rapidly to buttocks, then slowly lower.

Single Leg Curl
Lie on stomach in leg curl machine and kick one rapidly to buttocks, then slowly lower. Repeat with opposite leg.

Isometric Hamstrings Hold
Kneel on ground whilst partner holds ankles firmly. Lean body forward and hold for set period of time, before lowering. Repeat at varying angles.

Medicine Ball Leg Curls
Partner rolls medicine ball down back of legs whilst athletes kicks medicine ball back up and partner catches.

Backwards Running
Moving backwards in clear open space, rapidly kick heel to buttock region.

The following exercises are compound movements involving multiple joints – including the upper, mid and lower body.

Romanian Dead-lift

Hold barbell at waist height with normal or overhand grip. Lean forward lowering bar, with slight bend at knees until back parallel to ground, before raising. Ensure abdominals braced at all times to protect lower back.

Straight Arm Clean Pull

Start with shoulders over bar on ground in flexed position. As the bar rises above knees, thrust the hips forward keeping the bar close to the body. As the lower body reaches full extension, shrug the shoulders whilst keeping the arms straight.

Snatch Pull

Start with shoulders over bar on ground in flexed position. As the bar rises above knees, thrust the hips forward keeping the bar close to the body and continue pulling up. As the lower body reaches full extension, shrug the shoulders and pull bar up towards shoulders.

Power Clean

Start with shoulders over bar on ground in flexed position. As the bar rises above knees, thrust the hips forward keeping the bar close to the body and continue pulling up before rapidly flexing the

elbows to bring the body under the bar and resting bar across front of shoulders.

Power Snatch

Start with shoulders over bar on ground with snatch grip in flexed position. As the bar rises above knees, thrust the hips forward keeping the bar close to the body and continue pulling up to near maximum height whilst pulling the body under the bar in a semi-squat position with the bar above the head and arms locked out.

Single Arm Dumbbell Power Clean

Start in a squat position with dumbbell extended down between legs in one hand. Pull up and thrust hips forward keeping the dumbbell close to the body before rapidly flexing the elbow to bring the body under the dumbbell to semi-squat position before standing up.

Power Bounding

Bound forwards using long strides for set distance only whilst good form can be maintained.
Variation: Diagonal Bounding

Note: See Movement Pattern 4: Squat for additional drills.

Chapter 7

Movement Pattern 4

Squat

Functional Squat Progression

Gluteal Region
- Often referred to as the buttock region, the primary function is hip extension in unison with the hip stabilizers important in all lower body movements.

Quadriceps
- This is the large group of muscles on the front of the upper leg, often referred to as the thighs. Their primary function is to flex the hip and extend the knee.

Hamstrings
- This is the group of muscles on the backside of the upper leg, running from the hip joint to the knee joint. Their primary function is to facilitate flexion of legs, medial and lateral rotation – important for walking, running and jumping.

The following exercises focus on the Movement Pattern = Squat.

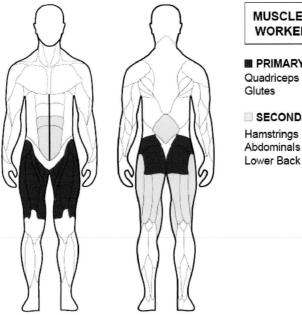

MUSCLES WORKED

■ PRIMARY
Quadriceps
Glutes

□ SECONDARY
Hamstrings
Abdominals
Lower Back

Key Movement Pattern = Squat

Start   **Midpoint**

Instruction
- Stand with feet shoulder-width apart, arms extended forward and parallel with ground.
- Establish foot arch, knee and hip alignment.
- Apply 3B's principle™.
- Breathing in, simultaneously bend the knees and lower body pushing the gluteus back whilst shoulders remain over knees.
- Maintain neutral balance and alignment through ears, shoulder, knees and feet.
- Breathe out and rise upwards to complete one repetition.
- Perform the exercise in a slow and controlled manner focusing on good alignment and body position at all times.

Note: Avoid the knees or toes rolling in or heels lifting by keeping the weight across the arch of the foot and good alignment through the ear, shoulder, knee and toes.

Variations include: quarter, half and full squats

Supported Squat – Learning Good Squat Technique

Start   Midpoint

Instruction
- To assist with squat development, stand next to a pole.
- Stand with feet shoulder-width apart, holding pole with both hands.
- Establish foot arch, knee and hip alignment.
- Using hands as a support guide only, simultaneously bend the knees and lower body pushing the gluteus back whilst shoulders remain over knees, and knees over toes – trailing the hands down pole with your body.
- Keep head close to pole when lowering and focus on adjusting body to maintain a good body position – ear over shoulder, over knee, over toes.

Note:
- Using a pole enables you to improve the technical aspect of squatting and is a great warm-up exercise. Once competent, move away from pole and repeat the squat movement using one's body weight only.
- Master this drill before adding any weight to the squat exercise.
- Regular stretching and massage is important for maintaining good muscle pliability for all exercises.

Functional Fitness Progressions - low to high intensity.

Apply 3B's Principle™ with each exercise. Refer to Functional Fitness Progression Table (on page 23) for additional variations of intensity and technical aspects for these exercises.

Squat Movement Variations Include – quarter, half and full squats

Fitness Ball Squat

Rest fitness ball against wall and the arch of the lower back, with feet shoulder-width apart and arms extended forwards. Breathing in, simultaneously bend the knees and lower body pushing the gluteus back whilst shoulders remain over knees, into squat position before rising.

Bodyweight Squat

Stand with feet shoulder-width apart and arms extended forwards. Breathing in, simul-taneously bend the knees and lower body pushing the gluteus back whilst shoulders remain over knees into squat position before rising.

Medicine Ball Squat

Stand with feet shoulder-width apart and medicine ball held against chest. Breathing in, simultaneously bend the knees and lower body pushing the gluteus back whilst shoulders remain over knees into squat position before rising.

Dumbbell Squat

Stand with feet wide and arms extended down holding single dumbbell with both hands. Breathing in, simultaneously bend the knees and lower body pushing the gluteus back whilst shoulders remain over knees into squat position with dumbbell touching ground before rising.

Medicine Ball Push Press

Stand with feet shoulder-width apart and medicine ball held against chest. Breathing in, simultaneously bend the knees and lower body pushing the gluteus back whilst shoulders remain over knees into squat position. Upon rising extend the medicine ball up overhead.
Variation: Squat, push and release

Kettlebell Front Squat

Stand with feet shoulder-width apart and kettlebell held high against chest. Breathing in, simultaneously bend the knees and lower body pushing the gluteus back whilst shoulders remain over knees into squat position before rising.

Kettlebell Rear Squat

Stand with feet shoulder-width apart and kettlebell held high on upper back to challenge the body's center of gravity. Breathing in, simultaneously bend the knees and lower body pushing the gluteus back whilst shoulders remain over knees into squat position before rising.

Squat with Weighted Plate

To challenge the core and shoulder region whilst performing a squat, stand with feet shoulder-width apart and weight plate held out parallel to ground. Breathing in, simultaneously bend the knees and lower body pushing the gluteus back into a squat position, whilst lowering the weight plate, before rising and raising arms.

Barbell Quarter Squat

Stand with feet shoulder-width apart and bar behind neck. Breathing in, simultaneously bend the knees and lower body pushing the gluteus back whilst shoulders remain over knees into a quarter squat position, before rising.

Barbell Rear Squat

Stand with feet shoulder-width apart and bar behind neck. Breathing in, simultaneously bend the knees and lower body pushing the gluteus back whilst shoulders remain over knees into a half or full squat position, before rising.

Barbell Front Squat

Stand with feet shoulder-width apart and bar resting across front of shoulders. Breathing in, simultaneously bend the knees and lower body pushing the gluteus back whilst shoulders remain over knees into a half or full squat position, before rising.

Barbell Squat to Overhead Press

Stand with feet shoulder-width apart and bar behind neck. Breathing in, simultaneously bend the knees and lower body pushing the gluteus back whilst shoulders remain over knees into a half or full squat position, before rising and extending arms up overhead.

Barbell Squat Push Press

Stand with feet shoulder-width apart and bar resting across front of shoulders. Breathing in, simultaneously bend the knees and lower body pushing the gluteus back whilst shoulders remain over knees into a half or full squat position, before rising and extending arms up overhead.

Fitness Ball Single Leg Squat

Rest fitness ball against wall and the arch of the lower back, with one foot extended forwards with arms. Breathing in, simultaneously bend the knee and lower body pushing the gluteus back whilst shoulders remain over knees, into squat position before rising. Vary depth to suit strength and stability levels. Repeat opposite leg.

Single Leg Squat

Stand on one leg with the other extended and raised and arms reaching forwards. Breathing in, simultaneously bend the knee and lower body pushing the gluteus back whilst shoulders remain over knees, into squat position before rising. Vary depth to suit strength and stability levels or use pole for support. Repeat opposite leg.

Single Leg Squat Foot Hold

Stand on one leg with the other extended and held by hand. Breathing in, simultaneously bend the knee and lower body pushing the gluteus back whilst shoulders remain over knees, into squat position before rising. Vary depth to suit strength and stability levels or use pole for support. Repeat opposite leg.

Kettlebell Single Leg Squat

Stand on one leg with the other extended and hands holding kettlebell in front of the body. Breathing in, simultaneously bend the knee and lower body pushing the gluteus back whilst shoulders remain over knees, into squat position before rising. Vary depth to suit strength and stability levels. Repeat opposite leg.

Overhead Barbell Squat

Start with the bar above the head in a wide grip position with the arms locked out and feet positioned outside of shoulder-width. Descend by allowing the hips, knees and ankles to flex to half or full squat position while keeping the knees aligned over feet before rising to the start position.

Kettlebell Single Arm Squat Push Press

Start with kettlebell resting on shoulder. Descend by allowing the hips, knees and ankles to flex to half or full squat position while keeping the knees aligned over feet before rising and extending the arms overhead. Repeat opposite arm.

KB Double Arm Front Swing

Stand in wide stance with kettlebell extended down in front of body held in both hands. Initiate movement by swinging the kettlebell backwards through legs, keeping the back flat and weight on heels, then up in front of body whilst rising, before squatting again and repeating for desired time or reps – only with good form.

KB Single Arm Front Swing

Stand in wide stance with kettlebell extended down in front of body in one hand. Initiate movement by swinging the kettlebell backwards through legs, keeping the back flat and weight on heels, then up in front of body whilst rising, before squatting again and repeating for desired time or reps – only with good form. Repeat opposite arm.

Squat Jumps

Lower body into squat position before driving arms and body up off the ground bringing knees to chest before landing, absorbing force and repeating.

Variations: Standing long jump test, Vertical jump test; Multiple jump sequence.

Functional Lunge Progression

Gluteus Maximus (buttocks)
- Extend and outwardly rotate hip and extend the trunk.

Quadriceps
- This is the large group of muscles on the front of the upper leg, often refered to as the thighs. Their primary function is to flex the hip and extend the knee.

Hamstrings
- This is the group of muscles on the backside of the upper leg, running from the hip joint to the knee joint. Their primary function is to facilitate flexion of legs, medial and lateral rotation – important for walking, running and jumping.

The Lunge exercise compliments the Squat exercise by introducing multiple planes of movement for strengthening the mid and lower body regions. These variables include: front, side, rear, diagonal, walking, forwards step-up, multiple stair climbing, lateral set-ups and step over's onto more power based plyometric drills.

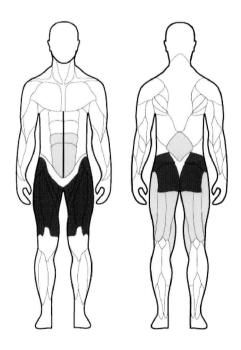

MUSCLES WORKED

■ **PRIMARY**
Quadriceps
Glutes

☐ **SECONDARY**
Hamstrings
Abdominals
Lower Back

Key Movement Pattern = Lunge

Start   Midpoint

Instruction
- Stand tall, feet together hands on hips.
- Apply 3B's principle™.
- Breathing in, step (lunge) forward and slowly lower your body by bending your knees to approximately 90-degree angle – keeping your knees aligned over your toes and your pelvis square.
- As your rear knee reaches near the ground breath out and push back up to the upright starting position.
- Keep tall through the chest and aim to make movement flow efficiently.
- Repeat desired repetitions on one leg, and then the other.

Arm variations: To challenge each exercise, vary your hand positions, for example, hands on waist, arms by side, arms extended forwards, arms overhead and so forth, before adding a resistance to the hands and once again performing each drill using these varying hand positions to increase the exercise intensity.

Master the basic lunge sequence before adding sideways, diagonal or backward leg movement patterns as shown on the following pages.

Functional Fitness Progressions - low to high intensity.

Apply 3B's Principle™ with each exercise. Refer to Functional Fitness Progression Table (on page 23) for additional variations of intensity and technical aspects for these exercises, namely varying hand positions to increase intensity. In each exercise ensure hips remain square at all times.

Stationary Leg Lunge

Stand tall in forward lunge position with hands on waist and resting on rear toes. Keeping torso tall and braced, bend knees and lower rear knee towards ground, before rising. Repeat drill with opposite leg forward.

Alternate Leg Lunge

Standing tall with feet together and hands on waist, lunge forwards into lowered lunge position before pushing back up to upright starting position. Repeat with opposite leg.

Side Lunge

Standing tall with feet together and hands on waist, lunge out to side into lowered lunge position before pushing back up to upright starting position. Repeat with opposite leg.

Diagonal Lunge

Standing tall with feet together and hands on waist, look diagonally turn and lunge into lowered lunge position before pushing back up to upright starting position. Vary diagonal movement directions using both legs.

Backwards Lunge
Standing tall with feet together and hands on waist, lunge backwards into lowered lunge position before pushing back up to upright starting position. Repeat with opposite leg.

Walking Lunges
Standing tall with feet together and hands on waist, lunge forwards into lowered lunge position and then continue forwards again, lunging with the opposite leg over a set distance.

Hand Weight -
Six Lunge Variation
Utilizing the above six exercises, add hand weights to each movement to increase the intensity of each exercise. In addition, vary the hand position to further increase the core demand.

Weighted Overhead
Alternate Leg Lunge
Stand tall with feet together and hand weights resting in front of body at shoulder height. Lunging forwards, simultaneously raise arms up overhead before pushing back up to upright starting position and returning hands to shoulders. Repeat with opposite leg.
Variation: Hands above head at all times.

Medicine Ball Lunge Rotation

Stand tall with feet together holding medicine ball in front of the body. Lunging forwards, simultaneously rotate arms across forward leg before pushing back up to upright starting position. Repeat with opposite leg.
Variation: Holding weight plate or kettlebell

Medicine Ball Single Arm Lunge Press

Stand tall with feet together, holding medicine ball in one hand at shoulder height. Lunging forwards, simultaneously push arm up overhead, before pushing back up to upright starting position and returning hands to shoulders. Repeat with opposite arm and leg.

Kettlebell Stationary Lunge Cross Overs

Stand tall in an upright stationary lunge position with one hand holding kettlebell by your side. Descending into a lowered lunge position switch kettlebell under leg into opposite hand and up and over leg and you rise back to starting position. Repeat movement for set amount of reps before changing legs.

Raised Stationary Lunge

Stand tall in forward lunge position with back foot raised on flat bench and hands on waist. In a controlled motion, bend knees and lower down before rising. Repeat drill with opposite leg raised.

Fitness Ball Stationary Lunge
Stand tall in forward lunge position with back foot raised on fitness ball and hands on waist. In a controlled motion, bend knees and lower down before rising maintaining good core control. Repeat drill with opposite leg raised.
Note: Place ball against wall for extra support, if required.

Step-ups
Stand tall with feet together and hands on waist in front of flat bench. Step one leg up and then the other before reversing movement. Repeat drill with opposite leg.
Variation: Keep one foot on bench at all times and drive rear leg up. Add a sand bag across shoulders.

Single Leg Knee Drive
Stand tall with feet together and hands in running position in front of flat bench. Step one leg up and then the other raising knee up high in running motion before reversing movement. Repeat drill with opposite leg.
Variation: Keep one foot on bench at all times and drive rear leg up. Add hand weights.

Barbell Step-up
Stand tall with feet together and barbell resting across back on shoulders in front of flat bench. Step one leg up and then the other before reversing movement. Repeat drill with opposite leg.
Variation: Keep one foot on bench at all times and drive rear leg up.

Barbell Leg Drive

Stand tall with feet together and barbell resting across back on shoulders in front of flat bench. Step one leg up and then the other raising knee up high in running motion before reversing movement. Repeat drill with opposite leg.
Variation: Keep one foot on bench at all times and drive rear leg up.

Kettlebell Side Lunge

Stand tall with feet together holding two kettlebells in both hands by your side. Lunge out to side into lowered lunge position before pushing back up to upright starting position. Repeat with opposite leg.

Kettlebell Lunge Switch-Overs

Stand tall with feet together holding kettlebell in one hand by your side. Lunge forwards with opposite leg to hand and switch kettlebell under leg before rising and repeating sequence on opposite side.

Barbell Stationary Lunge

Stand tall in forward lunge position resting barbell across rear of shoulder. Keeping torso tall and braced bend knees and lower rear knee towards ground, before rising. Repeat drill with opposite leg forward.

Barbell Alternate Leg Lunge

Standing tall with feet together and barbell resting across rear of shoulders, lunge forwards into lowered lunge position before pushing back up to upright starting position. Repeat with opposite leg. **Variation:** Walking, backwards, diagonal

Kettlebell Lunge with Single Arm Press

Stand tall with feet together, holding kettlebell in one hand at shoulder height. Lunging forwards, simultaneously push arm up over-head, before pushing back up to upright starting position and returning hand to shoulders. Repeat with opposite arm and leg.

Stair Lunges

Stand in front of stairs. Lunge forwards 2-4 steps at a time depending on your limb length maintaining good body posture leaning forwards. Avoid over-stepping to avoid poor body positioning. Ensure core is held strong at all times.

Lateral Step Overs

Stand sideways to bench with hands on waist. Step one leg up on bench followed by the other before stepping down across the opposite side. Repeat drill from other side up and over again – up, up, down, down movement.
Variation: Hold sandbag across shoulders for added resistance

Lateral Power Drives

Stand sideways to bench with one leg raised on bench and arms by side in running position. Rapidly drive off raised leg and swap with the opposite leg.

Variation: Hold sandbag across shoulders for added resistance

Power Split Lunge

Standing in an upright forward lunge position with arms by side, lower down and rapidly explode up off ground swapping legs in mid-air before landing. Repeat opposite side.

Variation: Multiple jumps

Medicine Ball Power Lunge Jumps

Standing in an upright forward lunge position holding medicine across forward leg, lower down and rapidly explode up off ground swapping legs and arms in mid-air before landing. Repeat opposite side.

Chapter 8

Core

Functional Core Progression

Rectus Abdominus
- Flex the trunk

Obliques
- Rotate, flex, side bend trunk. Support viscera and assist exhalation.

Iliopsoas
- Flex hip

Abdominal exercises are often progressed through a series of core-isometric bracing and breathing drills to build static postural endurance. This is then followed by a series of muscular contraction exercises involving the abdominals and obliques as well as Iliopsoas and lower back region, collectively referred to as the core region.

The following exercises focus on the Movement Pattern = Core.

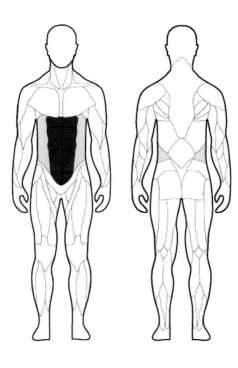

MUSCLES WORKED

■ **PRIMARY**
Abdominals

▢ **SECONDARY**
Obliques

Key exercise: Body Dish - Supine

Start   Raised

Instruction
- Lie in an extended position – legs together, toes pointed; arms overhead, hands together.

Dish Holds
- Simultaneously raise legs and arms into dish position and hold, ensuring deep breathing and strong abdominal brace is maintained for a set period of time (i.e. 5 or more seconds).

Repetition Based
- Lie in an extended position – legs together, toes pointed; arms overhead, hands together.
- Bracing your core abdominal region, contract musculature and simultaneously raise arms and legs into a body dish (banana) position, then lower maintaining long streamlined body position without relaxing.
- Repeat movement for set amount of repetitions with good form.
- Breathe out as you rise up (dish) and breathe in as you lower.

Note: This exercise includes use of abdominal muscles, ilipsoas and isometric involvement of the legs with toes pointed.

Functional Fitness Progressions - low to high intensity.

Apply 3B's Principle™ with each exercise. Refer to Functional Fitness Progression Table (on page 23) for additional variations of intensity and technical aspects for these exercises, namely varying arm positions to increase intensity and holding a weighted object.

Abdominal Arm Slide to Knees

Lie on back with knees bent and hands on thighs, sliding hands up to knees, then lowering.

Abdominal Crunch with Arms Across Chest

Lie on back with knees bent and arms crossed, raising shoulders off ground, then lowering.

Abdominal Crunch with Arms Behind Head

Lie on back with knees bent and hands behind head, raising shoulders off ground, then lowering.

Overhead Abdominal Crunch

Lie on back with knees bent and arms extended overhead, raising shoulders off ground, then lowering.

Fitness Ball Crunch with Arms Forwards

Lie on fitness ball with arms extended forwards. Contracting abdominal muscles, rise up into crunch position, before lowering.

Fitness Ball Crunch with Arms Across Chest

Lie on fitness ball with arms crossed. Contracting abdominal muscles, rise up into crunch position, before lowering.

Fitness Ball Crunch with Arms Behind Head

Lie on fitness ball with hands behind head. Contracting abdominal muscles, rise up into crunch position, before lowering.

Overhead Fitness Ball Abdominal Crunch

Lie on fitness ball with arms extended overhead. Contracting abdominal muscles, rise up into crunch position, before lowering.

Single Leg Dish

Lie on back with arms extended overhead, one leg bent and the other extended. Contracting abdominal muscles, simulaneously raise arms and legs into dish position, then lower. Repeat with opposite leg.

Body Dish

Lie on back with arms and legs extended. Contracting abdominal muscles, simultaneously raise arms and legs into dish position, hold, then lower.

Variation: Isometric or repetitions

V-Sit

Lie on back with arms and legs extended. Contracting abdominal muscles simultaneously raise arms and legs into v-sit position, then lower.

Medicine Ball Toe Touch

Lie on back with legs raised and arms extended holding medicine ball in hands. Contracting abdominal muscles, raise medicine ball to feet then lower.

Medicine Ball Trunk Raise with Toe Touch

Lie in extended position on back with legs raised and arms extended holding medicine ball in hands. Contracting abdominal muscles, raise medicine ball up to feet then lower.

Elbow to Knee

Lie on back with one knee bent and the other raised across thigh with opposite hand behind head. Raise elbow towards knee, then lower. Repeat opposite side.

Elbow to Knee Leg Crunch

Lie on back with one knee bent and the other extended with opposite hand behind head. Simultaneously bend knee and raise elbow towards knee, then lower. Repeat opposite side.

Medicine Ball Elbow to Knee

Lie on back with one knee bent and the other raised across thigh with opposite hand holding medicine ball on shoulder. Raise medicine ball towards knee, then lower. Repeat opposite side.

Medicine Ball Elbow to Knee Leg Crunch

Lie on back with one knee bent and the other leg raised with opposite hand holding medicine ball on shoulder. Simultaneously bend knee and raise me-

dicine ball towards knee, then lower. Repeat oppo-site side.

Side Raises

Lie on side with lower arm extended and upper arm forward of the body for support. Simultaneously raise arm and legs then lower in rapid and controlled motion. Repeat opposite side.

Medicine Ball Twists

Sit on ground with legs slightly bent holding medicine ball in hands. Lean slightly back and brace abdominal muscles. Slowly twist medicine ball from knee to knee.

Variations: Partner catch and thrust; throw and catch against wall (advanced only)

Collins Functional Rotation – 180-degrees

In dish position, roll onto side then stomach and hold, before reversing movement. Repeat in opposite direction.

Collins Functional Rotation – 360-degrees

In dish position, roll onto side then stomach, other side then back in a 360-degree rolling motion main-taining good form. Repeat in opposite direction.

Collins Functional Ball Rotation – 180-degrees

Lie on fitness ball across back and shoulders with arms extended out wide. Rolling arms to left side, cross left foot under right and out wide, whilst rolling across fitness ball onto stomach to complete 180-degree role. Repeat drill in opposite direction.

Collins Functional Ball Rotation – 360-degrees

Lie on fitness ball across back and shoulders with arms extended out wide. Rolling arms to left side, cross left foot under right and out wide, whilst rolling across fitness ball onto stomach. Continue rotation by taking right foot across to return onto back once again, for 360-degree rotation. Repeat drill in opposite direction.

Fitness Ball Knees to Chest

Lie in front support position resting feet on fitness ball. Bring knees to chest by rolling feet in and out.

Fitness Ball Single Knee to Chest

Lie in front support position with one leg resting on fitness ball and the other raised. Draw single knee to chest by rolling foot in and out whilst keeping hips square. Repeat opposite leg.

Kettlebell Raise

Lie on back with knees bent and one arm extended up holding kettlebell. Using abdo-minal muscles raise arm and shoulder up of ground, then lower. Repeat using opposite arm.

Kettlebell Raise to Foot

Lie on back with one leg bent, the other leg raised and slightly bent and opposite arm extended up holding kettlebell. Using abdominal muscles raise arm and shoulder up of ground towards opposite foot, then lower. Repeat using opposite arm.

Kettlebell Toe Touch

Lie on back with legs raised and arms extended holding kettlebell in hands. Contracting ab-dominal muscles raise kettlebell up to feet then lower.

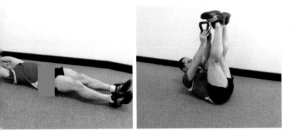

Kettlebell Raise with Toe Touch

Lie in extended position on back with legs raised and arms extended holding kettlebell in hands. Contracting abdominal muscles raise kettlebell up to feet then lower.

Cable Diagonal High Pulls

Stand sideways to cable machine gripping handle in both hands beside the body. Pull cable up and across body, before returning to starting position. Repeat on opposite side.

Cable Diagonal Rotations

Stand sideways to cable machine gripping handle in both hands beside the body. Simultaneously pull cable across body whilst rotating feet in direction of movement, before returning to start position. Repeat on opposite side.

Front Raise with Isometric Abdominal Challenge

To challenge the core and shoulder region whilst performing a squat, stand with feet shoulder-width apart holding dumbbell in both hands out parallel to ground. Lower and raise dumbbell from waist to eye-line without any movement of the core.

Hanging Knees to Chest

Hold overhead bar with wide grip and legs extended down. Activate abdominal muscles and draw knees to chest, then lower. To avoid swinging have partner hold lower back, until you become stronger.

Variable: Use Captains chair with lower back support and forearms resting on pads close to body.

Hanging Vertical Leg Raise

Hold overhead bar with wide grip and legs extended down. Activate abdominal muscles and draw feet and straight legs up to bar, then lower. To avoid swinging have partner hold lower back, until you become stronger.

Arm Hold Sequence 1 – Balance

In a squat position rest elbows on inside of knees. Lean body forward on ground and balance on hands for set period of time.

Arm Hold Sequence 2 – Balance to Front support

In a squat position rest elbows on inside of knees. Lean body forward on ground and balance on hands. Brace abdominals and kick legs up and out into front support position.

Arm Hold Sequence 3 – Diagonal Hold

In a squat position rest elbows on inside of knees. Lean body forward on ground and balance on hands. Brace abdominals and kick legs up, holding 60-degree static angle keeping arms bent.

Variation: Rise up to handstand.

Medicine Ball Power Abdominal Thrust

Lie on back with knees bent and medicine ball held in both hands overhead. In one motion, crunch abdominals whilst raising arms and thrusting ball forwards to partner who catches and rolls back to you.

Variation: Partner throws back, you catch lower and thrust again.

Medicine Ball Power Rotational Thrusts

Stand sideways 2-5 meters from solid concrete wall with medicine ball to side. Rotate arms across the body to release medicine ball across to wall then catch and repeat movement across the body. Repeat opposite side.

Variation: Stand 4-6 meters from wall; thrust ball, allow to bounce before catching and repeating to reduce eccentric loading.

Medicine Ball Power Throw Down

Stand tall with medicine ball extended overhead. Simultaneously jump up as you thrust the ball down to the ground in front of the body. Land, then catch ball after initial bounce.

Chapter 9

Movement Pattern 6

Movement Fitness

Movement Fitness = Speed & Agility

In this instance, Movement Pattern 6 focuses on movement fitness in terms of speed, agility, reaction and quickness. As speed is a combination of frequency of stride rate and stride length, improvements in running technique and skill levels can produce dramatic gains in speed. The following areas will help guide you to better movement fitness when used in combination with speed specific and interval training:

Speed Resistance

Resisted Functional Movement Patterns

Speed resistance involves sprinting in multiple directions whilst being resisted, using equipment such as harnesses, weighted vests, parachutes and running uphill. The resistance you place on a muscle causes it to work harder and may assist in recruiting more muscle fibers. Care should be taken to ensure the correct level of resistance is applied. Light to moderate resistance achieves greater functional gains making the specific running muscles stronger.

Functional workout example:

* Distance: 5m - 40m
* Repetitions: 4 – 8
* Recovery Period: 1 – 3 minutes

Note: The type of drill, level of fitness and training experience will influence the distance, rest periods and volume of weekly sessions. Rest periods should be long enough to ensure near full recovery between repetitions if speed development is to be maximized.

Speed Sled

Instruction: A weight plate is placed onto the speed sled to suit the athletes training requirements. Attach harness around body and secure. Using an open grass area or running track drive forward in strong running position for set distance of 40m-80m.

Parachute

Instruction: Attach harness around body and secure. Using an open grass area or running track drive forward in strong running position for set distance 40m-60m whilst parachute provides resistance.

Weighted Vest

Instruction: The weighted vest has varying increments of weight that can be adjusted to suit an athletes training age or ability level. Place vest around torso and tighten accordingly. Using an open grass area or running track drive forward in strong running position for set distance whilst vest adds extra resistance to the running drill.

Resistance Harness

Instruction: Attach resistance harness around body. Coach stands behind and grasps handle. Using an open grass area or running track drive forward in strong running position whilst the coach provides light resistance. After set distance of resistance (ie. 10m) the coach lets the athlete go, to sprint forwards for 20m-40m.

Overspeed

This involves a neurological adaptation to training with a focus on making the muscles more quickly using training equipment such as an elastic harness or by running down gentle slopes. It is vitally important, that with both of these methods, correct form and posture is maintained otherwise it is harder to transfer the benefits to a real athletic situation.

Overspeed Training Cord

Instruction: Both athlete and coach attach harness around waistline. Athlete extends training cord to full length back away from coach between markers. On go, the athlete sprints forwards whilst the coach continuously pulls the cord forwards, ensuring the cord is out of the way of the runner. The overspeed effect requires the athlete to adjust accordingly whilst sprinting. The athlete then decelerates after passing the coach who follows.

Note: There are many types of overspeed cords. Aim to use them at different angles in resistance and overspeed situations, where appropriate for agility gains.

Speed Endurance

In pure speed training, sessions may not involve sprinting any further than distances of up to 60 meters, where as speed endurance sessions may involve sprinting over distances of 100 - 200m. Sessions are designed around high quality work including sprinting shorter distances and having longer rest periods. As the athlete develops, the distances are increased and the rest periods reduced. Once a good speed base has been established, it is important to develop speed endurance so that a high speed can be maintained over longer distances. Speed endurance is best completed as a separate session or at the end of another speed session, if time is restricted.

Agility

Agility involves being able to move quickly over short distances in multiple directions. Agility can be developed by trying to replicate movements that occur in a sporting situation. This can be achieved by using equipment such as speed ladders, markers, mini hurdles and agility poles. Acceleration and deceleration are two important elements of agility training that imitate a sporting event. Although agility drills do not always reflect the reactive and decision-making qualities that are required in a game situation, they are a great way to imitate the demands of the sport at high speed whilst focusing on posture and good technique.

Functional agility example:
- Time on task: 5-10 seconds
- Drills: 10 Reps in circuit format
- Recovery Period: 30-60 seconds

Marker Rapid Lateral Steps

Equipment: 6-10 Markers, 1 meter apart in a straight line

Description
- Stand side-on and lead into markers laterally at speed.
- Zig-zag legs forwards and back laterally through markers.
- Repeat in opposite direction.

Variation: Run forwards stepping in and out of markers.

Agility Pole Evasion Drill

Description
- Position 6-10 agility poles 1-2 meters apart in a straight line.
- Lead into agility poles at speed.
- Step across and forward through agility poles as quick as possiible.

Variation
1. Forward swerve with lateral call to sprint (ie. run forwards through agility poles then on coaches call turn left or right and sprint 10m).
2. Lateral running through agility poles.

Speed Agility Drill

Three markers are set 5-meters apart on a straight line.

Instruction
- The athlete starts at the middle marker.
- On go, the athlete moves to the left side marker, touches it, and returns past the middle marker to the far marker and touches it before returning back to the middle marker once again.

Note
- The layout can be also be increased to 10m between each marker.
- Specific forwards, sideways and backwards movements can also be incorporated.

Mini-Hurdle Run Thru's

Description
- Position 6 (to 12) mini-hurdles up to 1 meter apart in a straight line.
- Stride through placing one foot between each hurdle using an efficient running motion.

Variation
- Run through the hurdles and sprint out when reaching the end.
- Gradually increase hurdle spacing distance to promote acceleration and stride length.

Mini-Hurdle Leg-Overs
Description
- Position 6 (to 12) mini-hurdles up to 1 meter apart in a straight line.
- Stand laterally and outside the of line of hurdles.
- Moving in lateral direction raise straight leg up and over hurdle.
- Land forward leg and repeat with trailing leg moving laterally along hurdles.
- Continue pattern, then repeat in opposite direction with opposite leg leading.

Acceleration Ladder
Description
- Space acceleration strips to set distance for longer stride length.
- Start with short fast feet in each grid, moving into longer steps and sprinting action.

Variation
- Lateral steps with step-out into forward sprint – adjust grid distances accordingly.
- Accelerate out of ladder into full sprint.

Speed Ladder Lateral Cross-overs

a. Right foot in box

b. Left foot in box

c. Right foot outside box

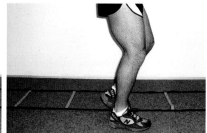

d. Left foot touch

e. Right foot outside box, left foot in

f. Left foot touch and step out again

Description
- Start at the front of the ladder to the left side.
- Enter the right foot into the box forwards at a 45-degree angle, followed by the left foot. Then, step the right foot out of the box and sweep the left foot across keeping the foot off the ground.
- With the weight on the right foot, angle the left foot into the next box and repeat above action along ladder.

Kettlebell Get Up

Instructions
- Lie on your back with kettlebell raised in one arm overhead.
- Keeping the arm locked out at all times, pivot on the opposite side on body using free arm to push up onto knee in semi-lunge position before rising up onto feet.
- Maintain vision on the kettlebell at all times to ensure smooth transition.
- Reverse movement pattern lowing down.
- Swap hands and repeat movement up and down again.

Reaction

Reaction refers to the time lapse between the presentation of a stimulus and the first muscular contraction – for example – when a sprinter leaves the blocks. Reaction time can be improved by practice, provided that the practice conditions are similar to the actual requirement of the sport. The ability to move the body quickly from a stationary position is demonstrated in the falling start drill:

Falling Start

Stand tall   Lean forward   Reac and sprint

Description
- Stand tall with feet together and hands by your side.
- Lean forward and raise up onto toes until balance is lost.
- React with two quick steps and rapid arm drive followed by short sprint over 10-20 meters.

Functional Medicine Ball Drills

Performing specific power drills enables the body to align synergistic fluency between muscle groups by improve strength, power and the appropriate response with the Central Nervous System (CNS). The following medicine ball drills aim to assist with body awareness and motor coordination allowing muscles to fire quicker and more efficiently.

Squat Thrust

Start   **Squat**   **Explode**

Instruction
- In a clear open space, stand between markers holding medicine on chest in both hands.
- Breathing in, gently squat before exploding the legs and body up off the ground whilst thrusting the medicine ball forwards, away from the body.
- Ensure you land correctly on both feet with legs shoulder-width apart and arms by your side for balance.

Overhead Thrust

Start | Squat | Thrust Overhead

Instruction
- In a clear open space, stand with back to direction of thrust.
- Stand with feet shoulder-width apart between markers and arms extended down in front of the body holding medicine ball.
- Bracing abdominal muscles, simultaneously squat down and then extend legs and arms up thrusting and releasing ball overhead and behind the body.

Plyometric Power Drills

Plyometric power drills involve exercises where an eccentric muscle contraction is quickly followed by a concentric muscle contraction. In other words, when a muscle is rapidly contracted and lengthened, and then immediately followed by a further contraction and shortening, often referred to as the stretch - shortening cycle.

Kangaroo Hops

Instruction
- Set mini-hurdles or markers 1-2 meters apart over 10-15 meters.
- Hop forwards on both feet, up and over markers.
- Upon each landing, take off quickly upward again with the same cycling hop action of the legs – use arms for balance and control.
- Execute the action sequence as rapidly as possible.
- Work on speed of movement, but not at the expense of poor technique.
- Maintain good body posture at all times when jumping and landing as quality of movement is paramount over quantity.
- Perform 3 sets of 6-second explosive movements; rest 90-180 seconds between sets to ensure high quality movements.

Single Leg Speed Hop

Instruction

- Stand on left leg next to marker, legs slightly bent and arms by side.
- Start with counter movement – squat, swing arms backwards.
- Hop forwards on left leg.
- Upon each landing, take off quickly upward again with the same cycling hop action of the legs – use arms for balance and control.
- Use the multiple-response action of rapid yet fully explosive cyclic action for height and distance.
- Perform single leg hop over 20 meters.
- Maintain good body posture and technique at all times when jumping and landing as quality of movement is paramount over quantity.
- Rest 3 minutes and repeat using right leg.

Note: Record differences in both legs in terms of time, technique and amount of steps taken over 20m distance. Aim to improve balance between legs.

Coach Collins™ Static Stretching Sequence

To assist with static stretching drills I have developed a series of static stretching cycles that flow together to ensure each working muscle is targeted. Each cycle follows a specific order of stretches flowing from one muscle group to the next, one after the other. Every stretch is held for 15-30 seconds and the cycle itself can be repeated 1-3 times. Most importantly, adapting these cycles as part of a normal training session will help increase athlete proprioceptive awareness and provide essential muscular skeletal feedback. Ensure an effective cool down has been performed prior to performing the following cycles.

Coach Collins™ Static Stretch Sequence – Cycle 1

1. Adductors
With feet together, gently push down on knees with elbows.

2. Hamstrings
Rest one foot on top of the other with legs straight. Keeping arms straight and fingers cupped extend arms behind body. Gently lean forwards from hip.

3. Hip, Gluteal and Spine

Cross one leg across the other resting foot on ground and gently twist behind.

4. Gluteal

From above (no. 3) release arms, keep legs where they are and lie back lifting legs off the ground. Reach one hand through legs and the other hand outside and grab front of knee and pull legs towards chest and hold.

5. Mid and Lower Back

Release arms and lower legs to ground twisting hips to one side and opposite arm to the other.

Repeat the above sequence using the opposite leg to complete one cycle.

Coach Collins™ Static Stretch Sequence – Cycle 2

1. Psoas
Kneel on ground pushing hips forward. Rest leading forearm across forward high and reach other arm backwards.

2. Thigh
Grab rear foot and pull towards glutes whilst pushing hips forwards.

3. Hips and Gluteal
From above (no.2) lean to side resting across shins and keeping shoulders square. Straighten back leg and cross behind body as you lean forwards.

4. Calves

Raise into front support position and rest toes on rear heel to stretch calf muscle.

Repeat the above sequence on opposite leg, followed by the following stretches (5-6) to complete one cycle.

5. Lumbar Extension and Abdominals

Lie on stomach on elbows and forearms and gently raise chest off the ground to stretch abdominals and lower back.

6. Thoracic Extension

Kneeling back extend arms forward and hold.

Note: : Additional Static Stretches for all major muscle groups can be located in The Body Coach® Stretching Basics Book.

Functional Fitness Exercise Index

Chapter 8: Movement Pattern 5: Core

Movement Fitness = Speed and Agility

The Body Coach® –
Products and Services

BOOK SERIES

The Body Coach® Book Series
- The Body Coach provides the latest cutting edge fitness training books written in a user-friendly format that is so advanced, that it's actually simple.

SEMINARS

The Body Coach® Keynotes and Seminars
- Corporate health and wellbeing keynote presentations
- Convention partner programs
- Seminars and Workshops
- Exclusive 5-star VIP Coaching – World-wide
- TV, Radio, interactive and Print Media Services

COURSES

The Body Coach® Programs and Courses
- Personal Training Certification Courses
- Continuing Education Courses (CEC)
- Licensed Group Fitness: Fastfeet®, Quickfeet®, Posturefit®, Swimstrength™, Kidstrength™
- Weight Loss Programs – Thigh Busters®, Belly Busters®, 3 Hour Rule®

PRODUCTS

Body Coach® Fitness Products and Brand Licensing
- Product Range – Speedhoop®, Spinal Unloading Block™, Muscle Mate®, Lumbatube™, Itibulator™, Rebound Medicine Ball™ & more...
- Product Education – Book and DVD Productions
- Product Brand Licensing opportunities

www.thebodycoach.com

International Managing Agent

Saxton Speakers Bureau (Australia)
- Website: www.saxton.com.au
- Email: speakers@saxton.com.au
- Phone: (03) 9811 3500
  International: +61 3 9811 3500

www.thebodycoach.com

Photo & Illustration Credits

Cover Photo: dpa – Picture Alliance
Cover Design: Jens Vogelsang
Other Photos & Illustrations: Paul Collins/Mark Donaldson

The Body

Paul Collins
Core Strength

Core Strength features practical, easy-to-follow exercises to help you build your strongest body ever using your own body weight. The Body Coach, Paul Collins, provides step-by-step coaching with detailed descriptions of over 100 exercises. As a substitute for lifting heavy weights, Core Strength provides body weight exercises for strengthening, toning and reshaping every major muscle group in the body and staying in shape all year round.

ISBN: 978-1-84126-249-9
$ 17.95 US
£ 14.95 UK/€ 17.95

Paul Collins
Awesome Abs

The abdominal muscles serve a critical function in daily movement, sport and physical activity. A strong mid-section helps support and protect your lower back region from injury. Better Abs for All is packed with over 70 easy-to-follow exercises and tests aimed at achieving a leaner abdomen, a stronger lower back, better posture and a trimmer waistline. You'll not only look and feel better, but athletes will find that a well-conditioned mid-section allows them to change direction faster, generate force quicker and absorb blows better.

ISBN: 978-1-84126-232-1
$ 14.95 US
£ 9.95 UK/€ 14.95

Paul Collins
Speed for Sport

Speed is the number one factor linked to improving athletic performance in sport.
Paul Collins' unique coaching guides you step-by-step through increasing speed for sport.
The book offers over 100 of the latest speed training drills used by world class athletes and sporting teams for developing speed, agility, reaction and quickness.

ISBN: 978-1-84126-261-1
$ 17.95 US
£ 12.95 UK/€ 16.95

Hintergrund: © Neliana Kostadinova - Fotolia.com

MEYER
&MEYER
SPORT

www.m-m-sports.com

Coach

Paul Collins
Strength Training for Women

The combination of strength training, aerobic exercise and healthy eating habits has proven to be most effective for fat loss and muscle toning. Strength Training for Women has been developed as a training guide as more women begin to understand the health benefits of this activity. A series of strength training routines for use in the gym as well as a body weight workout routine that can be performed at home are included.

ISBN: 978-1-84126-248-2
$ 14.95 US
£ 9.95 UK/€ 14.95

Paul Collins
Power Training

For many years, coaches and athletes have sought to improve power, a combination of speed and strength, in order to enhance performance. Power Training is designed as an educational tool to assist in the development of training programs that aim to keep athletes fit, strong and powerful all year round. 80 power training drills, tests and training routines are included which have also been used by Olympic and world class athletes to improve their performance. Power Training is an excellent guide for conditioned athletes to increase and develop their jumping, sprinting and explosive power.

ISBN: 978-1-84126-233-8
$ 14.95 US
£ 9.95 UK/€ 14.95

www.thebodycoach.com